THE Buffalo Wolf

PREDATORS, PREY,
AND THE
POLITICS OF NATURE

THE Buffalo Wolf

LU CARBYN

SMITHSONIAN BOOKS • *Washington and London*

COPY EDITOR: Anne Gibbons
PRODUCTION EDITOR: Ruth G. Thomson
DESIGNER: Janice Wheeler

Library of Congress Cataloging-in-Publication Data
Carbyn, Ludwig N., date
The buffalo wolf : predators, prey, and the politics of nature /
Lu Carbyn.
p.   cm.
Includes bibliographical references and index.
ISBN 1-58834-153-4 (alk. paper)
1. American bison—Predators of—Wood Bison National Park (Alta. and
N.W.T.). 2. Wolves—Ecology—Wood Bison National Park (Alta. and N.W.T.).
I. Title.
QL 737.U53C275   2003
599.773' 097123' 2—dc21   2003041445

British Library Cataloging-in-Publication Data available

Manufactured in the United States of America
10 09 08 07 06 05 04 03   5 4 3 2 1

⊖ The paper used in this publication meets the minimum requirements of
the American National Standard for Information Sciences—Permanence of
Paper for Printed Library Materials ANSI Z39.48-1984.

FRONTISPIECE: Two young wolves in Wood Buffalo National Park
in September

To Anneli, Christa, Jaynne, Shellie, and Carol

Contents

Apparitions

in the Mist

Completely isolated, I relished the solitude of being in a tent near a ribbon of water bearing the unlikely name of Lousy Creek. It flowed through one of the most remote places on earth, Wood Buffalo National Park. Located along the border of Alberta and the Northwest Territories of Canada, it is a place insignificant to, even neglected by, most of the world. My nearest neighbors were in Fort Chipewyan, a small native village two days away by canoe. There was no radio, no telephone, no television, no sound of any human voice other than my own. It was a happy time. I was alone, and life was full of adventures. This was the life I had dreamed about and that by good fortune had come my way. The roots of my being there lie in my childhood.

As a young naturalist and aspiring scientist, I spent my youth wandering through acacia savannas on the family cattle ranch in Southwest Africa (now Namibia). I was always searching for adventures and usually searching alone. The nearest farmhouse being many miles away and with no playmates next door, I was a loner. It was a basic life. Water was delivered once a week by donkey cart. No electricity—only kerosene lanterns and candles. I remember as a youngster going to the kraal, an African name for the fenced-in area around a watering hole for cattle. Water in that parched landscape was precious, thus it attracted a variety of wildlife. I spent many hours there observing birds and mammals. On one particular day a warthog came menacingly close. I had seen warthogs before, but this one was only a couple of paces away, coming right at me. I panicked, escaping by climbing a fence post. Only later did I realize I had been in no danger; the animal likely had not seen me. But I was ten and my reactions were quick. Encounters like that, at an early age, probably conditioned my later ability to feel completely at ease in wild and remote areas. A feeling of safety, I have come to realize, is connected to familiarity with the environment.

I discovered the beauty of nature and its challenges in the vastness of the African veldt. It was a wild place, a place filled with exotic birds and large insects, a land of extreme contrast: lush green grasslands after the rains and dust bowls during periods of drought. It was in this place that I began to formulate a strategy for some day becoming a zoologist. Those formative years would lead to a lifelong association with animals around the world, with a particular emphasis on carnivore research in temperate and sub-arctic regions of North America.

A slight breeze stirring the naked aspen branches woke me from my contemplation. The only worry I had in the wilds was my back and for now it was healthy. As I pushed open the flaps of my tent, a wall of dense, cold fog obscured my view. The warmth in my tent invited me to linger longer in my reminiscing. But it was time to explore the outside world; early morning is the best time to see wolves and bison. My reasons for being in Wood Buffalo, a name affectionately given to this national park, were simple—to study wolf predation on bison and learn how bison defend themselves against wolves. Along the way, I learned much more.

I reached for the pants that had served as a pillow, slipped them on, and crawled out into the fog. Wanting to get an early start, I had prepared breakfast and lunch the night before and placed them into my day-pack. The pack was stashed in a corner of the tent within a bear-proof container. I reached for it and made a quick exit into the mist. The fog obliterated the landscape. I reached out and although there was nothing but air, this nothingness was so thick that the willow bushes, only meters away, looked like dendrites on a frosted window pane. But I knew exactly where I was, recognizing the turns in the bison trail rutted by decades of trampling. The bison follow this trail to move from one meadow to another. Wolves use the same trail to follow the herds.

Slowly and silently I walked along, treading lightly on the soft, moist ground. The sun had not breached the horizon, or if it had, I could not yet see it. Not a whisper of a breeze stirred the air. Although I could see nothing, I expected that, once the cover lifted, I would find bison out in the meadows. And where there are bison, wolves are not far off. As I walked along, I smelled fox in a way you can only smell in the wilderness, far from exhaust fumes or the purification of air conditioning. The night before, I had heard two wolf packs howling nearby, surprisingly close to each other. Studies elsewhere have shown that wolves normally are territorial. Here it appears other rules apply—or do they? Maybe the wolves are territorial but have a different way of defending their territories. Maybe they are territorial only at certain seasons and not at others. Maybe the members of different packs are interrelated.

Only the occasional wind, the willows, and the ravens are witness to much of what takes place in the world of wolves, bison, and the other elements that complete the fabric of this boreal ecosystem. All I could hope for was to glean snippets of information and to try, as best I could, to piece some parts of the puzzle together. With 365 days in a year and possibly 200 wolves in Wood Buffalo there could be as many as 73,000 wolf/bison days and 73,000 wolf/bison nights a year for a wolf to encounter a bison. I despaired to think that my observations would add up to only a fraction of those interplays. Moreover, each wolf has a personality and character of its own. The best I could hope for was to obtain brief glimpses, and mere glimpses would never be enough to piece together the entire puzzle. I clung to the happier

A wolf leaving a den site on a misty morning in May

thought that whatever I could learn would be new, would add to the little we know about the relationship between wolves and bison. And that morning I did indeed observe a chapter in the epic struggle between predator and prey.

I cannot recall having a premonition that something important was going to happen, but I do recall being particularly sensitized to the pulse of the moment. The bison herds put on magnificent displays of their presence in the landscape as an empty arena comes alive with a mass of black bodies. Flying overhead are the opportunistic, ever-present ravens. The wolves had large litters, and several evenings before I had watched a pack of twenty-eight animals at one of their activity sites near my camp. Conditions seemed ideal for observing the interaction between predator and prey. The trail I was following led to my favorite lookout. In time, the sun's rays began to warm the earth and penetrate the mist, gradually lifting the blanket from the meadow. In front of me I began to make out a small herd of bison. Thirty of them, mostly lying down, a few grazing. I watched as the air continued to clear. It was a peaceful scene, a good place to relax and eat my breakfast. I unshouldered my pack and pulled out the thermos of tea. Two ravens landed near the small herd. As they did so, I glanced off to the side, and there in the distance I saw a faint long line of black and recognized the familiar sight of a larger herd of bison. The mist still dominated the scene, but its solid grip on the land was loosening. The large herd of bison was coming my way, possibly two hundred head. I watched as they slowly moved to the south in a straight line.

Then I noticed a shorter, white line moving briskly toward the herd. Wolves. The bison began to run and as they did so the wolves picked up their pace. The wolves closed in, pulling alongside the bison and, shortly, I saw the black line split into two. Calves, the prime targets for wolves in summer, usually move to the center of the herd when the wolves are in pursuit. The wolves had succeeded in splitting the herd, exposing the calves. Well aware of the opportunity, the wolves pulled past the straggling herd and caught up with the back end of the leading herd, where the calves were. I saw the black and white streaks intermingling.

Meanwhile the herd in front of me appeared oblivious to the drama unfolding in the background. A few minutes later they too became embroiled in the melee. With wolves pressing hard, the large herd suddenly wheeled around and stampeded westward, directly toward the small herd and me. First came the lead cow, thundering in my direction at full speed, with the rest behind her. Then, dashing in and out, came the wolves. There were too many bison to count, although I tried. Except for the muffled rumble of hooves, both predator and prey were so eerily silent that it all seemed surrealistically mechanical. I saw wolves attempting to tear at the hindquarters of bison; I saw bison wheeling about to face the wolves and then running again in panic, leaving their hind parts exposed. I could feel my heart pounding in my throat. The closer the action, the more engrossed I became with the drama. It was primeval, cruel, and very real. There was no escape for me, no cover if I were to be surrounded by prey and predator. Nothing to do but wait and see.

The wolves isolated a large calf, almost the size of a yearling. Within minutes they were slashing and tearing at its hind end. In their frenzy they also attacked its front and middle. Most of the adult bison moved on but three cows made a vain rescue attempt. Soon they left the calf as well. It seemed that the victim's fate was sealed. The wolves and the calf formed a single, moving mass of bodies.

As the calf's stomach was ripped open, warm air from the body cavity mingled with the cold air around it, forming a halo of condensation around the wolves and the calf. That image was burned into my mind—both the beauty and the cruelty of the sight. The calf got up and lunged forward. This time a large wolf braced its hind legs firmly on the ground and clawed itself up onto the calf, gripping the calf's back with its teeth. The wolf repositioned itself, and once more I could see the teeth sink into the calf's rump. If the calf was in pain, or in shock, I could not tell. I could not hear any vocalization, no bleating, no cries of pain. Why? I am told that in captivity distressed calves vocalize a great deal.

Suddenly the action stopped. Inexplicably, the wolves slunk off, abandoning the injured calf, which now lay half hunched in a crouched position. It was bleeding from the back and head, and part of its abdomen hung open. Mortally wounded, I thought. I was perplexed. What had prompted the wolves to relinquish their meal, now so imminent? Was it my presence? I didn't think so. To this point the pack had ignored me altogether, so why would it suddenly interrupt its actions? Why this change in behavior?

Faintly at first, then louder, came the answer. Motorboats, two of them. Duck hunters on Lousy Creek. During part of every fall and spring, native hunters from Fort Chipewyan travel along rivers and creeks shooting ducks and geese. Although wolves have little to fear from duck hunters, they are terrified of anything motorized, probably a result of trappers on snowmobiles chasing them in open terrain during winter. The wolves dispersed over the meadow, some lying down, others moving about restlessly but unwilling to finish off the wounded calf. One wolf was licking blood from its front paw, the white fur around its muzzle smeared red. At this stage I could count the wolves: seventeen, all light colored. In the fall the packs are large like this; during the winter of their first year wolves suffer high mortality. Thus few of this year's pups are likely to see the next spring, and the pack will shrink.

After some time, four wolves returned to the injured calf. The calf had remained at the same location, exhausted, abandoned by the herd. These four wolves were evidently the boldest of the lot, perhaps dominant wolves or ones driven by a greater hunger. The other wolves held back, likely to recover their energy, trusting that the mortally wounded prey would soon lie still and be easy pickings. The foursome grabbed at the victim, which, once more, stood up in an attempt to defend itself. As they toyed with their quarry, much as a cat would do with a mouse, the bison herd returned, attracted by the injured calf. I thought it possible the calf had uttered a distress call, one the bison had heard but I had not.

The mist had dissipated by this time and sunshine was warming the landscape. The four attackers seemed to lose interest in the dying calf. The drone of the still-approaching motorboat became too threatening for them. A single cow deliberately and rapidly advanced, then sniffed the calf; in response, the youngster managed to rise to its feet. The cow was almost certainly the mother. Then the most heartrending sight unfolded before my eyes. The calf, injured as it was, began to follow the cow. It could manage to move only very slowly, head leaning forward and bent down to the ground. A few remaining wolves watched from a distance. Ravens were winging about, apparently confident that it would be only a matter of time before they would gorge themselves on this moving carcass. The cow and calf moved off into the aspen forest along Lousy Creek.

I sat in a daze. How tough and stoic the calf was. Although it suffered numerous wounds—bleeding all over the body, a large rip in the flank that almost disemboweled it, bites on the head, nose, rump, neck, and back—it had made no sound. I tried to master my feelings of pity for the animal. At this point I would have been happy to help end its misery, but in a national park, nature must be allowed to run its course unimpeded. I pondered what I had read about feelings of others under such circumstances. I remembered John Murray, from Fairbanks, Alaska, who had written about one of his frequent visits to Denali National Park, where he watched a caribou bull that had been attacked by wolves around six o'clock in the morning (again those early magical hours) flee into a river. Here, in deeper water, the caribou had a slight defensive advantage over the shorter-legged wolves. For five hours the caribou had remained in the water in spite of the fact that the wolves had earlier shredded portions of the hind legs and begun to disembowel the victim. Murray had left, finding it too dispiriting to watch the animal suffer; he could not bring himself to stay to the end.

Even if the calf in front of me could survive its injuries in the short term, it would almost certainly succumb to subsequent infections. Andrew Campbell, an experienced indigenous trapper from Fort Chipewyan, once explained to park officials that "the wolves got poison in their teeth." This bit of indigenous knowledge, passed along from generation to generation, rings unlikely at first. However, studies have confirmed that the "poison" carried on the teeth of carnivores are bacteria that cause blood poisoning. In evolutionary terms such a symbiotic relationship between predators and bacteria has survival value for both, much to the disadvantage of the prey, whose entire body rots from within. The resultant odor is so rank that it is noticeable from a distance, providing predators and scavengers a clear indication of the prey's whereabouts. I did not see the calf die, but I knew death was certain. Hard as it is to watch, death is the companion to life. Indeed, what is the alternative? Without the wolves, the bison would eventually die slow deaths due to starvation in a landscape with an over-abundance of bison and not enough food. Simple food chains such as this make for readily discernible cause-and-effect relationships.

Despite my extensive observations in the spring and fall of each year, I did not witness another complete predation sequence from initial chase to the known end until three years after that October morning. Previously my students and I had observed parts of many attacks, and some kills, from the air, but not on the ground. The next time I stood and watched a kill I had the company of filmmaker Jeff Turner and his assistant, Anton Pauw. Jeff and Anton were filming wolves and bison for the BBC. We had secured two years of funding and were working together as a team. Jeff was the mastermind of the operation; I provided biological know-how. Over the years the team effort resulted in two international and three Canadian films on wolves and bison in Wood Buffalo.

We had established three camps, each stocked with provisions, allowing us more flexibility to move with the herds. The most northerly camp was one of three surviving cabins at Sweetgrass Station. Our base camp was a wall tent located at the crossroads of several large migration trails 10 kilometers (6 miles) south on Lousy Creek. Here we were outfitted with all the essentials required for comfort, a propane stove, large metal boxes with food, radio communication, solar panels to recharge batteries, and our sleeping tents. Eleven kilometers (7 miles) farther south, we set up a fly camp. It was situated in an area where large herds of bison often congregated in June, an area bounded by different branches of Lousy Creek. I noted that the area was suitable for grazing and might be important to cow/calf herds because it afforded solid footing, which I thought would enable the bison to run faster when under attack from wolves. Soft footing gives the predator a distinct advantage. Bison find fertile sedge meadows throughout the Peace-Athabasca Delta of Wood Buffalo. As appealing as the sedges and grasses of the delta are, solid footing is hard to find, especially in spring. In the summer, relatively solid footing is available in some areas, allowing the bison to feed selectively. During winter the whole scene changes. Everything is frozen, and bison have access to areas not easily available in summer.

How soft soil can influence a kill sequence became very clear to me one day in early May. Jeff, Anton, and I had shifted the scene of our observations from base camp on Lousy Creek to the warden's cabin at Sweetgrass Station. I began the day at 5 A.M., getting up to scan the Sweetgrass meadows. The sky was a miserable gray; the air cold. I took a short walk and noted that some aspen clones were beginning to show a slight wash of emerging green leaves. Flocks of migrating geese graced the sky overhead. To the south, I spotted a herd of twenty-seven bison, with their calves, bedded down in the same location they had been the evening before. Too early, too cold, no wolves, a good time to preserve energy, I thought. I went back to bed. At 6:00 Jeff took a turn to check the meadows. Stepping outside and peering through his binoculars he found the herd bunched up, always a sure sign of wolves nearby. Then he spotted the wolves.

"Wolves are with the herd," he shouted as he rushed back into the cabin. Within seconds Anton and I rolled out of bed, grabbed our packs, cameras, and binoculars, and rushed out. In our initial approach we hugged the edges of aspen forest for cover. However, when the action began to move rapidly away from us, we hastily set up the massive tripod and camera in the open meadow.

We watched seven white wolves move at a steady pace toward the herd. Then they suddenly stopped, turned, and bolted in the opposite direction. This was strange behavior. Why run away from the intended victims? My first thought was that perhaps a competing pack had arrived to chase away the intruders. Casting my eyes about, I confirmed my hunch. A dark, long-legged wolf, off to the left was racing full steam ahead across the meadow toward us. The situation became clear. Our white pack was not fleeing from intruders but attacking them. Two of the larger wolves from the white pack had suddenly wheeled about and were in hot pursuit of a black wolf that shortly sped right past us with a large "block-headed" white wolf on its tail. We subsequently named this large, pursuing wolf Rocky. Its head had a massive appearance. Rocky was to play an important role in the events that unfolded before our eyes for the next two and a half hours.

Rocky stopped some 150 paces in front of us (ignoring us completely) and looked at the routed black wolf. Head held high, tail up, Rocky stepped out in an assertive manner. He scent marked a willow bush, much like a dog would a fire hydrant. This animal was the boss and in control. To enforce the message he raked the delta soil with alternate heavy back and forth scratching of his hind legs, sending grass and dust flying through the air. Then Rocky turned to face the herd and began a long, low-pitched howl. The other pack members likewise turned in the direction of the herd. It was obvious from his disposition toward the others that Rocky was the alpha animal and other pack members responded to his leadership. I soon lost sight of the wolves; then I directed my attention to the herd, now some 2 kilometers (1.2 miles) away.

Jeff, meanwhile, had trained his movie camera on the herd. Peering through his 800-mm lens (affectionately known to us as "the cannon"), he announced that the bison were running. I looked for the wolves through my binoculars, but if they were there they were invisible among the tall sedges. I then noticed a single bison bounding off to the right. Following it through my binoculars proved difficult, but the animal appeared to be struggling. Then I saw white spots bobbing around it. Wolves slashing at their prey.

In less than five minutes the wolves had succeeded in covering the distance between us and the bison. They had isolated a victim, which was now falling behind the herd. I shouted to Jeff, "pan to the right." The moments seemed like an eternity as he tried to find the lone bison with his magnified lens, but he finally locked onto the frenzy of white specks lunging at and hanging from her stumbling black body. I could see the cow sinking into the mud, giving the wolves an edge in the struggle. The struggling cow tried hopelessly to rid herself of the attackers. "This is incredible," Jeff exclaimed.

Seeing and filming predator-prey interactions is much more difficult in the Canadian North than in Africa. Here it may take weeks before you see the predator, and to succeed you must spend many days lugging a heavy pack while camping in the open. In African parks, people simply drive in a Land Rover from watering hole to watering hole, watching hundreds, if not thousands, of prey animals daily. Camping is unnecessary there; interactions are commonly observed from the comfort of a vehicle, and nights are spent in resort bungalows. So too are visitors in Yellowstone National Park able to watch wolves and bison from the comfort of their campers parked along the road. There was no such comfort in Wood Buffalo. The area has a different character to it, and the opportunity to see and experience tooth-and-claw drama has to be acquired the hard way.

The hunt in front of our eyes seemed to us to be nearing its climax, but we were mistaken. The struggle had only begun. The alpha animals, those with greatest experience, were clearly the aggressors, the ones who persistently pressed the attack. The younger ones lagged behind but were not totally out of the action. We saw the wolves grabbing and slashing at the rear end of the isolated cow. This was, and remained, the intended victim. When the cow ran through a soft muddy area, the additional weight of the wolves, hanging onto her by their teeth, caused her to stumble and momentarily disappear out of our sight. It's over, I thought. But she must have regained her footing; shortly, she got up and again tried to run. The herd meanwhile had slowed down, and the cow, with her attackers hanging on, began to catch up to the others. Having found better footing and the cover of trees nearby, she seemed to have a renewed sense of hope. Momentarily she shook herself free from the determined attackers and galloped on. But the wolves, equally tenacious, caught up. Hanging on and slashing the hindquarters at a dead run, the adult wolves pressed the attack, the younger animals following behind.

The herd continued to run as the cow and wolves disappeared behind a stand of willows. This was our cue to gather our gear and follow. We sprinted after the retreating animals. Our course took us through the area in which the initial attack had occurred. While running, I noticed that the dry vegetation litter from the previous summer's growth made the footing consistently spongy. Below the litter was soft delta mud in which the running bison sank about 5 to 10 centimeters (2 to 4 inches). Not good footing for the cow; the wolves, being lighter, had an easier time of it.

The terrain where the cow had disappeared from our view led to a small, deep lake. I had camped here many times, so I knew it well. Because of its shape I had called it Banana Lake. Half an hour had elapsed from the time the wolves and the cow had disappeared from sight. We approached with care. Would the cow by now have escaped its attackers? Would we find the struggle still in progress? Or would the deed have been done—a carcass lying ripped open with hungry wolves devouring the still-steaming flesh? As it turned out, none of the above happened.

We saw the cow swimming in the lake, the wolves lining the bank. The wolves were excited, their tails wagging and their heads outstretched with ears erect. The cow, obviously weakened, was heading slowly toward a cut in the bank, a well-worn bison path leading in and out of the lake. This would be the safest, most familiar route. But her path was blocked. At the top of the embankment, about 1.5 meters (5 feet) above the water level, all seven wolves were prancing and milling around in anticipation. The alpha wolf was able to snap at the bison's face, almost, but not quite, tearing hair from the forelock area. The cow swung her head dangerously back and forth. One wolf, intent on making contact, actually began to slide down the slippery slope of the muddy bank but pulled back. It would have been deadly for the wolves to come any closer, and it was evident that the predators were well aware of such risks.

After a five-minute standoff, the cow staggered back into the water and commenced to swim in a wide circle toward a shallow point on the opposite shore. The wolves, circling around by the shore, confronted her again and forced her back into the water. Again, she headed back to the familiar cut-bank, the wolves arriving ahead of her. When she emerged from the water this time we could see the extent of her injuries. The soft area around the anus and tail had been ripped open and was bleeding. Because the water continuously washed off the blood, all injured areas appeared white, streaks of blood oozing from them. There were white tear marks on the flanks and hind legs, but her abdomen was intact.

Obviously trying to avoid a showdown, the cow once again retreated into the water, only to return to the embankment, her only possible exit. Although the lake offered a brief respite from the relentless slashing of teeth, it offered no permanent solution to her problems. She desperately needed to find a way to get back on dry land and rejoin the herd, which by now was long gone from the area. The wolves would not let her leave along the trail. Rocky was always the aggressor and moved back and forth, the others following his lead. The closer the cow came to leaving the water, the more aggressive the wolves became. We watched the drama repeat itself several times. In the background I could hear the whirr of Jeff's movie camera.

Finally the cow made a determined effort to get out of the water and past the wolves. Again the wolves denied her. All seven wolves attacked. She retreated into the water and started back to the opposite shore. This time the wolves launched themselves into the water behind her. Two wolves, Rocky and another dominant animal, dug into her back and ripped off pieces of flesh and hide as the threesome approached shore. Neither the wolves nor the bison vocalized, or if they did, we did not hear the sounds. When the cow left the water, the remaining five wolves took over the attack, while the two swimming wolves got out to consume meat successfully torn free. The wolves saw the cow, whether alive or dead, as food and would, if necessary, eat her a chunk at a time.

As the cow struggled onto the shore, the two dominant wolves positioned themselves in front of her, sidestepped the horns, and attacked the flank. For a few more seconds, it appeared that the bison still had strength left in her and kept the aggressors at bay, but when a third attacker arrived, ripping at the soft tissue, all her efforts were in vain. The force of the blow caused the victim to stumble back into the water. She made one final attempt to reach deeper water then, weakened and with wolves tearing and ripping at her from all sides, she simply stood, resigned to a fate she could no longer avoid.

Now the less-dominant wolves took over. Previously, Rocky had led the assault every time the cow attempted to leave the water. This time other pack members began to assert themselves, though we had the impression that all the wolves were less aggressive now, as if aware that the cow no longer had any chance to escape. The victim was visibly beginning to tire, her head defiantly shaking up and down as she attempted to gore her tormentors. She managed to walk several paces onto shore and the pack made its final assault. Her demise was imminent. The alpha wolf again tore at the soft tissue, dislodging a large piece and driving the victim back into the water for the last time.

Her movements were now so slow that she began to wobble and stagger. One wolf had jumped on the back of the cow and started to pull out tufts of hair, much as one would pluck the feathers from a chicken. Her strength was gone, her legs mired in mud. Three were tearing at her back and two at the shoulders. All the wolves, except Rocky, were feeding now. Rocky lay exhausted on the bank of the lake, watching with apparent satisfaction. When at last the victim collapsed, the young wolves, together with the other adults, converged on her. One young wolf climbed on top and tried to bite through the thick hide in the area around the side of the neck. Jeff, still glued to the camera, moaned loudly. "This is it, she is dying." His voice was breaking with emotion. "She is flailing her head in a last gesture of defiance, but it is going underwater." Bubbles blew from the cow's nostrils as her nose dropped below the water line. We had witnessed a drama seldom seen before. And I had learned a lot about wolf predation.

Members of the dog family employ a different strategy for killing their prey than do members of the cat family. The wolves we had witnessed killed their victim by pulling it down and commencing to eat even as it moved. Dogs in their many forms, wild or domestic, have longer jaws and more teeth than do cats. The longer jaws make the slashing-maiming process easier. In comparison, the claws and powerful forelimbs of cats enable them to pin down their prey as they deliver a killing bite. It may be a neck bite that cuts through the jugular or a suffocating jaw clamp that restricts airflow through the trachea or the nose. Generally, only when the victim has completely stopped moving will a member of the cat family begin to feed. Not so for canids.

Two and a half hours of this terrible yet gripping drama left us emotionally exhausted. Our sympathies (mine at least) were with the cow. Anton tried to subdue these feelings by directing us to a biological perspective. "Life is nothing but energy flow," he said. "Bison genes are simply being converted to wolf genes." Jeff, a most ardent wolf and wilderness enthusiast, was not so detached. "All the wolves could see in the cow was food," he lamented; "they offered neither rancor nor regret." I pondered another view. Even though humans tend to pass "good or evil" judgments on events such as these, morality has no place in the wild. Predators are part of the natural system; they too need to survive. In their survival lies the health of the ecosystem.

I knew from years of following the herds that we had been extremely lucky to have recorded this drama on film. This was a struggle of titanic proportions between the largest North American land mammal and the largest of the wild dogs on earth. As a result of our patience and persistence this drama could now be broadcast around the world. People sitting in the comfort of their homes around the globe (the film was shown in thirty countries) would be able to visit the delta for a few minutes and experience the brutal realities of this northern ecosystem. (As it turned out, in the final rendition of the film, this May encounter was presented as an autumn event to better fit the story line.)

Jeff unsnapped the camera from its tripod and the three of us, at once dazed and elated, wondered what we should do next. At my urging, we decided to move up closer, perhaps get some photographs of the carcass and foraging pack members. We did this, cautiously following a bison trail, mindful not to disturb the scene. When we were within about 120 paces, we took cover and I set up my 35-mm camera. However, the light was now poor and the angle too difficult for still photos. Instead, we watched quietly, curious how quickly the pack would consume the carcass, and made plans for follow-up work. We could have opted to spend the night with the carcass, but we decided against disturbing the pack and returned to camp.

The next day, cameras in hand, we arrived at the site at 5:30 A.M. Through the early morning mist we could see that about half the meat had been consumed and the pack had left. We built a blind nearby and settled in, hoping the pack would come back. Unlike the day before, it was quickly turning sunny and warm. We found out that the wolves had just left as we arrived. I saw one wolf in the distance moving away. It moved slowly with a noticeably distended stomach. Throughout the day's watch we observed only a single wolf, either a stray pack member or a lone wolf, approach and feed on the carcass. We decided to sleep at the site that night. While Jeff and Anton set up the camera, I returned to base camp to get our sleeping bags.

On my way to camp I was surprised to come upon a small reddish calf, wandering alone in the wide-open meadows. I thought it likely to be the orphan of the dead cow. Although I could not know for sure, all indications pointed toward this possibility. It kept heading back to where the mother had been killed. The cow herself, though thin looking, appeared healthier than several crippled animals we saw struggling behind the herd. I wondered why the wolves had chosen not to kill one of the crippled individuals. Perhaps the wolves had first targeted the calf but, upon noticing the cow losing speed in the mud, turned their attention to the bigger target. Maybe the wolves had other ways to sense the vulnerability of this individual. I suspect they did. After a brisk hike to camp, I returned to the kill.

We settled into our sleeping bags to keep warm. At sunset the wolves in the pack returned to feed on what was left of the carcass. Jeff was able to obtain excellent footage of the pack feeding, the sun setting in an orange glow behind them. On the second day we continued to watch over activities at the carcass. The wolves had evidently had their fill the night before, leaving behind a skeleton with bits of meat visible only on the underside of a submersed foreleg and on the head and neck area. The weather was cold and miserable, and we fought boredom as we sat and waited for hours on end for wolves that never appeared.

As dusk approached and we were about to give up, I spotted movement. Instantly we were attentive. Two white wolves, individuals we had not seen before, timidly approached the carcass and fed, nervously looking about for signs of the pack. They left in half an hour but later returned to feed for another half hour. We watched one of them swim across the lake toward what appeared to be a short piece of brown wood. We were astonished to discover that this was not wood, but a second carcass. A bull had drowned here, perhaps broken through winter ice or fatally injured by wolves. The water was too deep for wolves to find the footing necessary to pull the carcass ashore. Too deep for wolves, but maybe not for us.

If we could make this carcass available to the pack, I thought, we could continue to study the wolves and obtain more film footage. But how to move the body? In early May patches of snow persist and the water is ice cold. We looked at each other blankly, no one daring to suggest the obvious. Finally, Anton offered to swim out and tie a rope around the carcass. "Good idea," was my spontaneous reaction, and then I surprised myself by offering to join him. Jeff volunteered to stay ashore. Smart fellow.

Anton and I stripped off our clothes and began to wade out to the carcass. Deeper and deeper we went, the cold causing sharp pain. Chilled to the bone, I lost interest in the project when the water reached my chest. Anton, more youthful and zealous for adventure, continued on. Upon my return to shore, I snatched up Anton's clothes and streaked around the lake, ready to help warm him should he become hypothermic. I could now see only his head and, behind it, a small wake like that of a beaver. He was determined. Feeling guilty, I reentered the icy, muddy shallows to throw him a rope so we could pull the carcass toward the shore. From there we hoped to drag the carcass through the water to a good viewing location. The first trick was to secure the rope somewhere on the body of the bison. Anton was groping underwater, trying to locate the horns. A loud muttering indicated that his finger had slid into a soft, viscous, rotting eyeball. "God, Lu, this critter stinks," he protested. All the while treading water, he groped deep down for a leg but ended up with the tail. He tugged hard at something and came up with a slimy, mass of white tissue. Exasperated, he tied the rope to the tail and, pulling, managed to turn the carcass sideways. As it rolled, an oily, metallic slick exuded from the mouth, anus, and opened body cavity. As the slick closed around Anton I could hear new utterances of dismay: "I think I'm going to throw up!" I was not surprised. Even Jeff, who was on shore and some distance upwind, could smell the decay.

Preferring to be upwind of the carcass, Anton decided to tow it to the opposite side. This required still more swimming, through the deeper portion of the lake, and prolonged exposure to the icy water. Concerned, I headed back into the bone-chilling water to help Anton complete the task. The cold was razor sharp. In minutes that seemed interminably long we got to shallower water, where we could brace our legs in the mud. Finally, we succeeded in towing the carcass to shore some twenty-five paces from the first kill. We quickly dried off and put on our clothes.

I remained alone at the site that night as Jeff and Anton returned to the warmth of Sweetgrass cabin. It was cold and rainy. From about 2 to 4 A.M., I could hear crunching of bones. Something was chewing on the carcass of the cow kill but not at the rotting bull carcass we had dragged out of the lake. At dawn I strained to see if the wolves were still at the carcasses. But they had left. Then, I too headed north to the Sweetgrass cabin. Jeff and Anton were waiting for me with breakfast, eager to hear any stories I might have to tell.

We returned that evening, and at about nine o'clock action again came our way. Jeff had gone to film the sunset; I was positioned behind a blind; Anton was in his sleeping bag. I glanced sideways. There was Rocky, trotting along the bank of a stream, some thirty paces from me, looking, then moving up the bank to get a better view. Our eyes locked. There is nothing in nature quite like the fixed stare of a dominant wolf. To a subordinate wolf it is the cue to turn and slink away. The eyes and head pointed in my direction were fixed and motionless. I am not sure how long we stared at each other.

I glanced farther to my right and saw, one by one, the other six pack members walk below Rocky past me toward the carcass. Jeff returned and saw them, but Anton was unaware of their presence. I could hear him rolling around in his sleeping bag, trying to find a comfortable position on the ground so that he could fall asleep. He was resting on a bed of dried grass and aspen leaves, which made a crunching sound every time he moved. There was no way I could communicate my sighting of the wolves to him. They were just too close. The wolves, not comfortable with our presence, soon disappeared, and there was nothing for Jeff and me to do but join Anton at the camp and crawl into our sleeping bags. My sleep was light and sometime in the night I woke up to the sound of wolves feeding, snarling as they pulled at the carcass, cracking bones, and lapping nearby lake water. It was too dark for filming and soon I drifted back to sleep.

At one that morning the pack howled. All three of us awoke to it at the same time; instantly we were reminded that the wolves were just a few paces away. Calm prevailed and we drifted off again. Toward dawn the pack again awakened us with the eeriest, most powerful and full-bodied group howl I have ever heard. It penetrated each of us. I raised my head to get a view of the carcass and the wolves. It was first light, but all I could see were the rays of the sun trying to penetrate a cover of mist on the water. Ducks were flapping their wings and courting. I could hear the chewing sounds of muskrats feeding on the fresh, green spring vegetation sprouting at the water's edge. Where were the wolves?

I looked toward the carcass but was barely able to discern outlines, the drifting fog still too thick at the lakeshore. Somewhere in that milky mass was the pack. A few had already left, but one member howled. Then, through a break along the opposite shore, I saw Rocky, followed by three others, moving in a leisurely pace toward a clump of willows. What a marvelous sight, their big, powerful bodies, wolf genes converted from bison flesh propelled forward by the steady stride of their long legs. Rocky's color blended with the gray mix of last year's sedges and the wispy mist. The scene was surreal. The wolf stopped and looked our way, its large angular head with protruding orbitals clearly outlined against the drab background. Apparitions in the mist, I thought, something out of Thomas Hardy's *Return of the Native*.

I asked both Jeff and Anton to describe their initial reactions to the howl. I was surprised by the difference in their responses. Jeff was buoyed by the experience; he could see how howling could inspire in humans a deep fear, but to him it was a joyous outburst of vital energy. He had witnessed, better than Anton and me, all the gory details of the kill two days before through the powerful camera lens. For Jeff it was a family group howl communicating pleasure. Anton felt differently. The howl struck him as powerful, melodic, and primeval. He commented on its bloodthirsty, bloodcurdling, hair-raising dimension, its wicked dark magic. Although not the same, it reminded him of hyena vocalizations he had heard in Africa.

Four days later we found that the wolves, and probably other scavengers, had completely consumed the putrid meat of the bull. In contrast to the carcass of the cow freshly killed by the pack, which had meat still clinging to the bones, the long-dead bull was picked as clean as if the meat had been cooked and fallen off the bones. I was amazed to see how much meat the wolves had consumed. Despite the presence of bison in the area, it is not always a time of plenty for the wolves. I have seen lone wolves that were severely emaciated. Feast followed by famine is common in the life of a wolf. Indeed there is evidence that wolves can survive, though maybe only barely, for months without eating much food. That May, however, seemed like a time of plenty for the Lousy Creek pack. They were well placed along the migration trails of the herds moving from the wooded wintering areas along the oxbows of the Peace River to the calving areas along the banks of Lousy Creek.

The Park
and the Delta

2

T he sheer size and emptiness of parts of Canada is astounding. Many a visitor from Europe or other densely populated parts of the world marvels that one can fly for a long time over forested areas without seeing any evidence of human habitation. Nonetheless people, particularly in the recent past, have left their mark. The discerning eye can detect traces of human intervention when visiting Wood Buffalo National Park.

The park is larger than many countries, occupying 44,800 square kilometers (17,297 square miles) most of which is located in the province of Alberta. Within the park lies the Peace-Athabasca Delta, a flat open landscape where it is fairly easy to see the wolves and bison interact. There

The boundaries of Wood Buffalo National Park

are differences between this delta and the African deltas I have seen. The Okavango Delta along the Botswana-Namibian border is much richer in biological diversity, has many more human residents, and attracts more tourists. Wood Buffalo is a simpler, starker environment. The Peace-Athabasca Delta covers an area of about 5,000 square kilometers (1,930 square miles). To say that it is remote is an understatement. Fewer than eight hundred people visit this Canadian wilderness in a year, and excepting those I planned to meet, I never saw a visitor in the delta's back-country during my three-plus decades of studies in the park.

Summer camps of the Dene Nation, whose traditional

pursuits took them along trails, rivers, and lakes in this northern landscape, were once scattered here and there. Now, the natives too spend less time in the bush. Evolution of the native cultures has taken them from life in the bush into the twenty-first century. When I first visited the area in 1964, the northern residents were still closely tied to the land. Today only the elders still have a connection; most of the young have affinities elsewhere.

The small native village of Fort Chipewyan (population about twelve hundred) is located at the edge of the delta on the Precambrian rocks and along the shores of Lake Athabasca. It is a closed community. Though planes come in and out year-round and there is a 285-kilometer (180-mile) winter road to Fort McMurray, there is no road access in summer. Summers are fairly short, warm, and dry, with long days and temperatures up to 30°C (86°F). The fall is generally warm until late September. Winters can be (but are not always) moderate until December, after which temperatures drop to –40°C (–40°F) with a mean temperature of about –20°C (–4°F). By April most of the snow is gone. The main waterways (lakes and rivers) are usually ice-free by late May.

Even when I am not in the park, I try to keep in touch with what is happening there. Whenever I need information, I pick up the phone at my home in Edmonton and call my trapper friend Reggie McKay. Reggie is a classic northerner, down to earth and a great raconteur. His nickname is "Swan," a moniker he picked up as a youngster. He is of mixed heritage but identifies himself most closely with his native ancestry. Just as fluent in his native Cree language as he is in English, he calls himself a "blue-eyed Indian." Wolves he sees as vicious killers; bison he loves. If you ask Reggie about bison and wolves, he will start his reply "Mister Man" and then give you an earful about the need to reduce the number of wolves.

If one single element preoccupies people's imagination and thinking in the region, it is the large wood bison herds that gave the park its name. People in Fort Chipewyan love their buffalo. So it is natural that one of my first questions to Reggie is invariably "how are them buffalo doing?" It is "them buffalo" to Reggie, not "those buffalo." There is a subtle difference in meaning between "them" and "those." "Them" brings the animal closer to reality, into one's own sphere. "Those" removes the buffalo to a more remote location.

Bison are visible in the open delta, but that is only a small part of Wood Buffalo. The vast wilderness of the park contains bogs, forests, sandy ridges, karst topography, meandering streams, huge silt-laden rivers, and tracts of muskeg. An aerial view, looking northward from Edmonton, Alberta, to Wood Buffalo National Park, shows a transition from patches of prairie to aspen parkland. Farther northward solid coniferous forest prevails. A net of roads and seismic lines crisscrosses these forests, but as one gets closer to the park, these lines diminish until they finally disappear. The landscape represents the best there is of primordial Canada: a land scoured by retreating ice ages that developed a mantle of green and formed the basis for a boreal landscape that was eventually occupied by the northern bison and the buffalo wolf. The wolves of the delta are predominantly light colored, although color shifts do occur from time to time, a likely result of periodic invasion of tun-dra wolves into the region. One such invasion may have occurred in 1949 when barren ground caribou wintered for a time in the northeastern portion of the park. This has not happened for more than fifty years now, but I have found antlers from the last invasion. These buffalo wolves are large wolves, adapted for life in the cold north and finding most of their food in the form of bison. However their food source depends on regional distribution. Many areas in the region have few, or no, bison, and other prey species become important. My studies have brought me north on several occasions to study wolves in different systems.

I joined the Canadian Wildlife Service in 1967 and from 1978 to 1984 had a number of assignments in Wood Buffalo National Park. Up to 1978 my trips to the park, with one exception, had been to the area north of the Peace River. The exception, in 1968, was a trip to Fort Chipewyan. At meetings between park officials and natives, I was invited to present a talk on wolves. After 1984 I became increas-ingly interested in the area south of the river. The delta landscape south of the Peace River is dominated by water, with Lake Claire at its heart. Standing on its shores, one can see long distances in many directions and observe the earth's curvature at the vista's fringes. Here, mammals, mosquitoes, and mirages may suddenly appear and just as suddenly evaporate.

Lake Claire is a large shallow lake covering an area of about 1,456 square kilometers (562 square miles). Size varies with flooding conditions. At no point is it deeper than about 3.5 meters (11 feet), but lake water levels can fluctuate by a meter, depending on the overall water levels in the delta. On average more than 50 percent of this huge lake is less then 1 meter (3 feet) deep. The lake is an important transportation route into and out of buffalo country. But traveling by water has its risks. On windy days it can be treacherous, and on numerous occasions I had to face nature's wrath and either postpone travels or wait out storms on islands in the lake.

In much of the delta, everything the wolf does depends on the buffalo. The largest land mammal on the North American continent, buffalo are members of the Bovidae family. The name "buffalo" originated with early French explorers, who called them les Boeufs, meaning oxen. Over time the name apparently went through a number of changes ranging from "buffle" to "buffelo" and finally its present "buffalo." Bison, however, is the name preferred by the scientists—and I occasionally use the words interchangeably to the ire of my colleagues. To natives, buffalo have a deep spiritual connection. Any one who has spent time in buffalo country will appreciate why that is so. You can wait for days or even weeks in an area seeing nothing but empty space on the horizon. Then, off in the distance, herds become definable, until you see these large dark beasts, shuffling along, vocalizing, and revitalizing the landscape with "good fortune": food for the natives, study subjects for the biologist, and images for the filmmaker.

The bison themselves have an aloofness about them. Like flocks of birds, they come, stay awhile, then vanish again. It is not hard to understand why their arrival, seemingly from nowhere and bringing good fortune, would be connected to that of a great spirit bestowing a gift on its people. The buffalo is a North American emblem—of what was of symbolic importance to the original inhabitants, and later of waste as newcomers destroyed the vast herds. The northern herds were at the fringes of the continental population. Because of the remoteness and wooded nature of the terrain, many bison in the north escaped the fate of their southern cousins.

By the start of the twenty-first century, North American bison numbers had greatly increased. One estimate puts them at 350,000. More than 97 percent of this current population is in commercial or semicommercial livestock production. The once magnificent wild herds have been reduced to glorified domestic livestock—dehorned, manipulated, and fenced in behind barbed wire. But there are exceptions, notably the worthwhile efforts by one of North America's wealthiest people, Ted Turner. He has poured enormous resources into bringing back the bison to its original ranges in the western plains. It is not the old Wild West but as near a replication as is possible. Buying up smaller holdings and amalgamating them into a larger whole, he has reversed some of the negative impacts of European settlers. Prairie dog towns, once poisoned and destroyed, are being restored; swift foxes and black-footed ferrets are returning from the edge of extinction. A small step toward the creation of a "Buffalo Commons."

The idea of a Buffalo Commons was initiated by Frank and Deborah Popper. They suggested that with the exodus of rural people from the Great Plains failing farmlands could be restored to native grasslands to the benefit of native prairie ecosystems. Bison, and a whole host of associated members of that threatened ecosystem, could be part of that mega-restoration effort. Could wolves be restored in such a system? Biologically not a problem, but political realities for the foreseeable future dictate otherwise. For wolves, of course, cattle are prey. In the unfenced environments of Wood Buffalo National Park, the herds are wild, free, and hunted by wolves.

These herds are the best representatives of what was. But the Wood Buffalo herds are not without their problems. The first was the introduction of two exotic diseases, brucellosis and tuberculosis. The second was the mixing of plains bison with wood bison populations. Both were the result of human interference. The diseases were introduced as part of a highly misguided management program in the early part of the twentieth century, when one of the most extensive transfers of large mammals from one area to another occurred. Plains bison infected with cattle diseases were shipped from central Alberta to the southern portion of the Northwest Territories along the border into Alberta, a distance of some 1,000 kilometers (621 miles)— no ordinary feat. Consider the difficulty of rounding up 6,673 wild bison, loading them onto railroad boxcars, freighting them for two days to one location where these large-bodied animals were unloaded then reloaded onto barges and transported for two or three days (under ideal conditions) to their final destination. The barges came to a stop on the west bank of the Slave River and dumped their cargo onto land. Staggering to their feet, the liberated "wild cattle" found themselves in entirely new country. Dazed and frightened, they looked around, then many took off for lusher pastures. Some traveled south. Within months many had reached the rich sedge meadows of the Peace-Athabasca Delta, which at the time was outside Wood Buffalo National Park.

Steps were immediately taken to protect the newcomers. The park was enlarged to accommodate the bison. Environmental conditions were ideal, so much so that after five years numbers had increased to 7,500 animals and then after five more years to more than 10,000. This, in the absence of high wolf numbers but in the presence of infectious diseases they brought with them to the area. The newcomers (plains bison) readily mixed with the established wood bison. How different are plains bison and wood bison? Scientists have debated this issue at length. Natives too have their views. Size appears to be one factor. Wood bison tend to be heavier, have a larger hump, reduced front leg chaps (so some think), and less of a woolly bonnet.

To rescue what was still thought to be a pure element of wood bison, a project was undertaken to move bison located in a remote northeast corner of the park, known as the Nyarling River bison, out of the park and into the Mackenzie Bison Sanctuary some distance from the park and on the north shore of the Mackenzie River. The program in the mid-1960s was a huge success, but the growth of this population ushered in a new era: protect disease-free wood bison in the Mackenzie River Bison Sanctuary from the disease-rid-

A wood bison showing the characteristics of the northern bison (drawing by Wes Olson)

A plains bison showing the characteristics of the southern (Great Plains) bison (drawing by Wes Olson)

den hybrids in the park. Purists wanted to protect the Mackenzie River bison; others had another agenda: get rid of Wood Buffalo National Park bison to protect ever northward-expanding cattle-ranching activities and bison-ranching operations. Some also wanted to eliminate diseases in the park. The debate is seemingly unending.

Many initiatives followed; some executed, others only contemplated. The Canadian air force was to be employed in the mid-1950s to eradicate bison in the park. Then selective slaughter of diseased animals in the late 1950s and early 1960s was invoked as a partial solution. Much grander schemes were brought up in the late 1960s and again in the late 1980s, early 1990s. These efforts failed for many reasons, not the least of which was a lack of detailed information. Much was known about bison, less about the buffalo wolf. Wolves in portions of the park truly are "buffalo wolves" because they prey largely on the bison. Moose occur but only in clumped and patchy distribution. White-tailed deer are likewise patchy in distribution and uncommon in most parts of the park.

For an animal the size of a wolf to dispatch a bison is not an easy task. A bull can weigh up to 900 kilograms (almost 2,000 pounds). Bison are heavily muscled; the hide is thick and has to be penetrated by teeth while the wolf is at a dead run. Although wolves and bison appear to be about evenly matched in speed, they appear to differ in their endurance levels and acceleration rates. My impression is that wolves can accelerate more quickly but bison have greater endurance. Wolf canines are comparatively long, yet small considering the task they are put to; the daggerlike teeth are controlled by incredibly strong muscles anchored to solid bones in the skull. Wolves bent on killing do so with a tenacity and relentlessness that defies the odds. The wolf is not always the victor. Bison have defenses

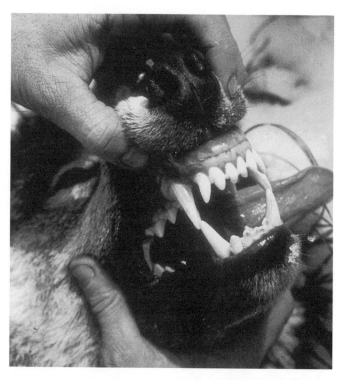

Daggerlike canines and incisors of a darted wolf (photo by
Sebastian Oosenbrug)

that allow enough of them to survive and perpetuate.
Spring and summer flooding in the delta may provide an
advantage for either wolves or bison; if water levels exceed
critical levels, the equation changes. What could be an
advantage in one season (warm-weather rain) can be a disadvantage in another season (freezing rain). Spring and
summer rains increase the lushness of the bisons' range,
but freezing rain on a snow cover forms a crust that makes

grazing for food sources difficult. A hard ice crust can cut the skin and cause abrasions on the legs of hoofed animals. Wolves have an advantage under those circumstances as they can travel more easily on the snow crusts while their intended victims are hindered in movement. Subtleties of events and evolutionary responses are so finely tuned that they can be easily missed. Seeing what is happening often takes time. My own development as a biologist has happened in stages over decades.

Before I began my wolf studies in Wood Buffalo National Park, I skied and snowshoed along trails in the valleys and alpine of Jasper National Park in Alberta, following the trails of wolves in the Canadian Rocky Mountains as they hunted for elk. In Jasper National Park I lived among the wolves using what has subsequently been defined as the "habituation technique." This technique was first brought to my attention by ungulate biologist Valerius Geist, who in turn had been inspired by a Swiss biologist, Heini Hediger. Geist's pioneering work was with bighorn sheep, and at the time no one had habituated wolves (although some had observed wolves in fairly close proximity). Habituation has a very simple premise: an animal is only as fearful of humans as humans' treatment of the animal. Reduce or eliminate the reasons for an animal to flee and the animal will not flee. In its simplest form, habituation is a process of "see" and "be seen." Put another way— the degree to which mammals are fearful of humans is a function of the degree of human persecution or harassment. The animal's flight response distance changes as familiarity increases and fear responses decrease. This technique is designed to overcome the study animals' fear responses. An animal that has no fear can be more easily studied, thus habituation allows observing, recording, and interpreting events in close association with the study animal. Geist taught me this lesson while he was still a graduate student. On a field trip with fellow students to Banff National Park, I sat perched on an elk corral fence post while Geist expounded on this concept. My professor, William (Bill) Fuller, led that trip. I was fascinated and intrigued and determined to try the technique on wolves. So began three decades of walking with wolves. It took two years, but eventually I habituated a wolf pack in Jasper National Park. In essence, I could sit among the pack and they would simply go about their business—grooming, fighting, howling, feeding pups, playing with sticks and antlers. I was simply a part of their environment.

The question I initially faced was how best to go about habituating a pack? What to do, considering that wolves are elusive and travel widely? Then too what would wolves do once habituated? Could they become a threat to me? In only a few cases have wolves proved to be a menace to human safety, and these isolated instances never resulted in the observer's death. I was not particularly concerned about a possible altercation—but no one ever wants to be the "celebrated" first. Habituating wolves sounded challenging, and I eagerly took up the cause.

The most logical approach was to find wolf dens or other sites to which wolves must return on a daily basis. Den usage, however, lasts for only a short time. After about four to six weeks wolves take their pups and establish activity sites (which wolf biologists call rendezvous sites), usually in fairly close proximity to the denning areas. Wolves spend much time at rendezvous sites from midsummer to late fall. Aerial photographs and a knowledge of site characteristics that wolves prefer allowed me to make some general predictions as to where the activity sites might be located. From here I narrowed my target by looking for concentrations of wolf tracks along trails and by listening to howling. Once I had located the animals themselves in Jasper National Park, I moved my camp, a small green tent, to a suitable location about five hundred paces from the rendezvous site.

After settling into my home away from home, I simply had to be patient. Any rash actions, unfamiliar noises, or sudden movements could provoke the animals into leaving. I was eager to have the wolves accept my presence as part of their environment, and this required my exposing myself to them gradually. To this end, I set up a schedule: going to an observation post at the base of a large tree for a brief period, then returning to my tent, gradually increasing the time spent at the observation post. I made a habit of walking along the same line from the tent to the observation post, thus allowing my movements to become predictable and less intimidating. At first, my encounters with members of the pack were only brief glimpses in dense vegetation. But in time, as my confidence and my observational abilities increased, I was better rewarded. Resting against the tree, I sat for hours waiting and listening.

I well remember my first close encounter with the Jasper Park wolves. Pups within a few meters from me. They were being fed by adults returning from a hunt. The whole pack was milling in front of me. It was early evening. The adults had announced their return by howling from a distance, prompting the waiting pups to respond with calls from the dense shrub cover that concealed them. Upon the adults' approach, the pups had come out into the open, in full view except for some willow cover and only about thirty paces away from my observation post. In subsequent encounters the distance was much less than that, without any cover. Clearly, with the Willow Creek pack of Jasper National Park, the process of befriending a wolf pack worked.

Two days later I caught glimpses of the adults as they moved like shadows among the trees. I had been waiting for twenty minutes when I heard the commotion of the hungry pups as they greeted the adults. Suddenly, the back of the alpha male, a large, long-legged wolf, appeared behind some low bushes nearby. The wolf stopped, then moved into the meadow, fearless of my presence. This was the first time I had seen a wolf unobstructed by any vege-tation within a few paces of where I was sitting. It was a defining moment in my life. I remember the excitement I felt watching this trim, wild animal eyeing me at close quarters. I was in a prone position, excitement coursing through my blood; I was annoyed at my heart for thump-ing so loudly and making it hard to concentrate. The wolf seemed to me to be completely habituated. There was absolutely no doubt in my mind that this adult male, and the rest of the pack, were aware of my presence. Wolves' sense of smell, hearing, and sight are highly developed, much more acute than those of humans. Yet it seemed that

Sights from

a Lofty Perch

Slowly I gained better insights into how the wolf-bison-delta system meshed together into a unit. The more work I completed, the greater my realization of how little we really understood about the dynamics of the system. Habituating wolves at a rendezvous site, I went to where the action was and became an observer. Sitting in a tower, I let the action come to me. Watching bison herds from a tower has advantages and disadvantages. Waiting for animals to appear can tax one's patience. But when the animals arrive the observer is well camouflaged and well positioned.

In the very beginning of my research program, back when the government was footing the bill, my students and

I built a 3-meter (9.8-foot) elevated, cabin-topped platform in an open area near the unimaginatively named Lake One. The cabin measured about 1.5 meters a side (5 feet by 5 feet). With a stove, food, sleeping gear, binoculars, scope, stopwatch, compass, and cassette recorder on hand, the observer effectively had a kitchen, bedroom, and office all in one place. We used it for three years. Thereafter, trappers used it as a place to have lunch or just to stop and look around and talk about those fly-by-night biologists who come and go and leave their structures behind.

It was here that one of those trappers was gored and killed by a bison bull, the first such recorded incident in Wood Buffalo. The trapper shot and wounded the bull, then went after the injured animal. The .30-caliber rifle was just too light to kill the animal. After traversing an open area, the hunter followed the bison through heavier vegetation cover where he was charged by the wounded bull. The goring was likely swift. Tracks in the snow indicated that the wounded man dragged himself, on his stomach, for about fifty paces and rested his head on his gloves. That is how the rescue team found him, frozen stiff, not far from his snowmobile. Tracks in the area indicated that wolves had been there as well. From personal experience I have found that to be a dangerous combination. Wolves can trigger aggression in bison. In the case of the fatal attack on the trapper, being wounded may have reinforced the bison's aggression and instinct for self-defense that was engendered by the proximity of wolves in the area.

In the late 1970s and early 1980s, bison herds regularly used the meadows along Lake One. My student Tim Trottier and I recorded an all-time high of twelve hundred bison sightings per week in June 1980 and a low of three hundred per week in July. Generally, the bulls preferred the meadows throughout summer, but only small numbers of them persisted here during the winter. Bulls were predictable and regular in their presence, whereas cow-calf herds seldom stayed long. During the rut, when mating takes place, cow and calf herds could be observed interacting with the bulls.

Two major factors influenced bison summer use of the Lake One meadows. These were the flood conditions in the delta and the local drought conditions. Prolonged dry periods reduced forage quality and inevitably forced the bison to search elsewhere. A simple measure of drought severity at Lake One was the presence of water in a watering hole near our observation tower. In 1978, a year of great bison numbers at Lake One, water was still present into late July, whereas by June 9, 1980, and June 2, 1981, the hole had dried up completely. The 1980 drought was accompanied by an explosion of grasshoppers. This was also the year that a pack of eight adult wolves raised six pups at a den near the observation tower. They used the den until June 26, permitting us to conduct behavioral studies. We watched this pack of "bison killers" all summer long and obtained unique insights into wolf personalities. Over time Tim and I recognized each wolf, and it was Tim who gave each pack member a name. These field names were based on the wolf's physical appearance, generally on the color of its fur. But as we learned more about each wolf, we were able to establish its social position in the pack and give it a name reflecting its status. The following list describes the wolves in the pack, using the status designation by which they are identified in the text; field names are given in parentheses.

Alpha Male (White-Gray) was the largest member of the pack. Overall, he appeared buff gray. His ears were reddish; black guard hair extended over the back, shoulders, and withers; and a conspicuous black streak extended along the front legs. Although his winter hair had been shed, Alpha Male's appearance was more full-bodied than that of the other pack members. Initial observations gave us the impression that Alpha Male was the only dominant male in the pack. Then New-Dark-Gray appeared on the scene.

Retired Alpha Male (New-Dark-Gray) was another large male, similar to Alpha Male in body coloration, but with a pronounced black mask. He was further marked by a distinctive black stripe extending from the tip of the tail to the shoulders. In overall form he appeared rangy and long legged. Although very domineering, at times appearing as the most dominant animal, Retired Alpha Male seemed to be less integrated into the pack's structure. He behaved as if he were "above" having to fit into pack society. The presence of two dominant males was of interest to us, particularly when situations arose that made it unclear who was really in charge.

Tagalong Male (Silver-Mane), another large male, was similar in coloration to Alpha Male but had a vertical, oblong dark spot on his left flank. He was smaller than Alpha Male and more slender, and he appeared long legged upon losing his winter fur.

Alpha Female (Black-Tail) was a small but dominant (alpha) female. She was almost identical to Retired Alpha Male in color and markings except that only about a quarter of her tail, near the tip, had a black stripe. Throughout the summer she seemed very "skinny," almost emaciated, possibly as a result of nursing pups.

Female Helper (Dark-Gray) was another female and resembled Alpha Female in coloration. Overall however, Female Helper was darker, lacked the sharp contrast between the face and sides, was smaller than Alpha Female, and had a more pointed snout with black on the side of the nose and chin area. She also showed a distinctive red coloration along her upper legs and flanks, and behind the ears.

Low-Ranking Female (Collared-Wolf) was a small, light gray female without outstanding coloration. This animal had previously been captured and was wearing a nonfunctional radio collar when we observed her that summer.

The Cripple (Lame-Wolf), whose sex we could not determine, was identified by its severe limp; its left front leg hung loosely at the joint and was thrown forward with each step. The physical disability did not appear to affect the wolf's position in the hierarchy. The wolf was gray in color, showing no outstanding coat patterns.

The Loner (Charcoal-Wolf), a small, light gray wolf of unknown sex, was seen only once during the summer. We considered it likely that it was an unaffiliated, wandering wolf drawn to the pack's Lake One hunting territory by the need to scavenge and possibly by an urge to connect occasionally with its own kind. This wolf was an interesting visitor and demonstrated the ability to temporarily "join the pack," but we did not consider it a full-fledged member.

The seven pack members were seen all together only once, in mid-May. Although, as is typical, the pack was a strongly bonded physical unit, its members were observed to hunt and travel most frequently in subpacks or as singles. Perhaps this physical separation induces the need to howl. Howling is the only way the pack can keep in touch and rejoin each other over the vastness of a pack's territory. Even though Alpha Male was the dominant male, we observed a curious relationship when Retired Alpha Male was present. Under such circumstances the latter appeared to dominate more often, which led Tim to conclude that there were two dominant males in the pack. In other words, they were codominant. We noted behavioral interactions, especially during attacks on herds, that suggested a complex set of subtleties that were not always easy to interpret.

Our first observation of a prolonged physical attack on a bison calf occurred on May 28, a day when Retired Alpha

The observation tower at sunset

Male was absent. In a series of encounters throughout the day, whenever the possibility of a kill presented itself, Alpha Male led the pursuit more frequently than Tagalong Male, Alpha Female, or Female Helper. Initially, the other wolves taking part in the raid paid more attention to the fleeing calf than to Alpha Male. I attributed their lack of cohesion to hunger. Alpha Male's prominence became more and more evident as the day wore on and the other wolves tired. By then, Alpha Male led the attacks almost exclusively and was the last to retreat. On at least three occasions he carried out the attacks alone, the others being out of range or holding back. Female Helper twice tested the herd alone, as the other wolves watched and rested. Tagalong Male generally followed Alpha Male's lead that day, venturing to head the charge only (and this rarely) when Alpha Male had momentarily dropped back. When Alpha Male gave up on an attack the others generally did likewise. Alpha Female frequently lagged behind the other wolves, joining them only during actual attacks or when they were resting. She seemed reluctant to press the bison.

Everything changed when Retired Alpha Male appeared on the scene. On June 3 we watched this "semi-retired" pack member interact with the other wolves. When first spotted, Retired Alpha Male and Low-Ranking Female were separate from the main pack. When Retired Alpha Male joined the relaxed company of Tagalong Male and Alpha Male, who were highly bonded to one another, Alpha Male immediately became more assertive. Field notes collected on June 17 further indicated the complexity of male dominance. Retired Alpha Male appeared in the meadow, leaving the den area, with Alpha Male following 250 paces behind. As they traveled southeast the leader stopped four times to raised-leg urinate, raise his tail, and scratch; Alpha Male stopped at each location and did the same. Raised-leg urination is usually reserved for the dominant males and, particularly when followed with vigorous, rhythmic, left-right turf scratching, is an assertion of dominance. On a sunny day and with dry ground this behavior scatters vegetation and dust and makes an unequivocal statement: "Take note, I'm in charge!" During the twenty-five minutes we observed the wolves, Retired Alpha Male was always in the lead.

A second indication that this essentially lone male was at least equal in status to Alpha Male came two days later, on June 19. Early in the morning we observed five wolves (the Cripple, Female Helper, Alpha Female, Alpha Male, and Tagalong Male) watching a mixed herd of bison three hundred paces to the south. Soon, Alpha Male got up and deliberately advanced toward the herd, walking slowly with his head lowered. Female Helper and Alpha Female followed closely while the Cripple moved up quickly from the rear with Tagalong Male behind him. When Retired Alpha Male howled once from the bush north of them, Alpha Female and Female Helper reversed direction and trotted toward the now-visible Retired Alpha Male. Tagalong Male and Alpha Male also broke off their pursuit of the herd but did not go to meet Retired Alpha Male. The Cripple and Alpha Female trotted quickly up to Retired Alpha Male, their tails low and wagging, reaching out to lick his muzzle. Retired Alpha Male then trotted off toward the others with Alpha Female and the Cripple following closely. Retired Alpha Male continued southeast and was followed shortly by Alpha Male, then Alpha Female and Tagalong Male. As they crossed the meadow, Alpha Male managed to take the lead for about fifty paces, but then dropped back again behind Retired Alpha Male.

Reflecting on this series of events, we thought it noteworthy that Alpha Male, Tagalong Male, and Female Helper had responded to Retired Alpha Male's call but did not approach him submissively as did Alpha Female and the Cripple. Also, Alpha Male appeared to initiate an attack on the bison herd but was then thwarted by Retired Alpha Male. Retired Alpha Male had successfully called it off. There was no question that the pack immediately changed its activity when confronted with just the howl of the "semiloner," a wolf not even integrated into the pack.

Eventually, all the wolves became submissive to Retired Alpha Male. Perhaps overplaying the human equivalency, I felt as if Retired Alpha Male were a respected elder in the pack, cherished for his wisdom. But how this wolf truly came to have such a strong hold over the pack, I could never say with certainty though Tim and I talked about it at great length.

On June 21 five wolves again had an opportunity to test a mixed bison herd. This time the harassment lasted for four hours. Initially, Retired Alpha Male led the attacks, with Alpha Male clearly following his lead. However, as the day wore on, Alpha Male became increasingly aggressive. Whereas all other wolves, including Retired Alpha Male, became disinterested and eventually abandoned the project, Alpha Male, although unsuccessful, continued the attacks on his own.

On another occasion we watched Retired Alpha Male launch a solitary attack on a mixed herd of bison, but to no avail. The next day Retired Alpha Male had more wolves with him, and the seven adult wolves attacked a mixed herd containing three calves. But this time, to our surprise, Alpha Male led the attack, charging past the trailing bulls. We witnessed a striking switch in leadership. Tagalong Male and an unidentified wolf trailed behind and were attacked by flanking bulls. They retreated. Soon Alpha Male terminated the pursuit. That day, further attempts by the wolves to kill a bison failed. Eventually, they succeeded in making a kill.

An observation on feeding sequences on a carcass illustrated the role that dominance played in wolf society—

wolf politics. Alpha Male, Female Helper, and Alpha Female were feeding on a bison calf killed early in June. When first spotted at 10:20 A.M., Alpha Male was resting twenty paces from the kill. His bloodstained face indicated that he had already fed. Female Helper and Alpha Female were feeding together and continued eating for ten minutes until both left to drink water. Shortly, Alpha Male and the dominant female, Alpha Female, returned to the kill. Only Alpha Female fed. When Alpha Female finished, Alpha Male then fed for thirty minutes. During our observations the most dominant male did not feed when other wolves were at the kill, and when he fed, he did so longer than any other wolf.

On August 24, we observed six adults and five pups at a kill. Initially, the wolves were prevented from consuming the calf by a bull, which through slow, deliberate, and threatening stances kept the wolves at bay. But the bull eventually gave up on the calf. Alpha Male did not immediately approach the kill; instead he watched while two pups fed first, followed by an unidentified adult. When Alpha Male finally approached to feed, all other wolves immediately abandoned the carcass and waited on the sideline. While he was feeding, Alpha Male was briefly joined by one adult and one pup, both of whom he tolerated. Then, about five minutes later, Alpha Male left and the other wolves descended in a free-for-all on the carcass. These observations indicated that this alpha wolf was generally intolerant of others feeding alongside him. Such behavior is variable and depends a great deal on the personality of the individual wolf.

It would have been interesting to see the interaction between Alpha Male and Retired Alpha Male, when both were hungry at a carcass. Likely Retired Alpha Male would have prevailed. All observations considered, I concluded that Retired Alpha Male really was the super alpha male, but for unknown reasons he was an emeritus pack member. He carried substantial weight when he showed up, effectively becoming the superboss, but wasn't troubled by the day-to-day responsibility of leadership. One needs to take care in interpreting such observations in human terms, as motivations in animals are not necessarily governed by the same rules as in humans. Yet it makes thinking about interactions easier if they are seen in similar terms. And some drives are comparable. Hunger is hunger, whether human or animal.

A den site, the hub of pack activity, was not visible to us from the Lake One tower. The tower's location also prevented us from consistently seeing the interactions among pack members and the pups. By deduction we knew that the den must be in a small open area surrounded by heavy vegetation cover. The movements of wolves to and from this site, and frequent howls there, clearly indicated its central importance. Eventually, my curiosity got the better of me and I decided to get a closer look at the den.

I left the tower in the late afternoon, a time I felt would be least disruptive to the pack. I approached cautiously, mindful of the wind direction and of keeping the sun behind me. In my experience, if you have the sun at your back, you apparently present a less identifiable image than if the sun is shining on you from the front. The dense bush made it hard to get a clear view without getting quite close; I was within 20 paces when I finally spotted the pups. As I had hoped, no adults were nearby. Alerted to my approach, two pups scurried to the entrance, hesitated briefly, then entered. I estimated they were eight weeks old, which meant they would have been born some time in mid-to-late April. Since my disturbance had been minimal, the adults did not relocate the pups, and I decided that, with a cautious approach, I could do this again. I wanted to know when the pack would abandon the den and move the maturing youngsters to their first rendezvous site. Rendezvous sites, first described for wolves in Ontario's Algonquin Park, are places where packs move the pups after leaving nursery dens. In this instance, a rendezvous site was selected about a thousand paces from the den. It was located in a low-lying area of three small meadows that were separated from each other and from the main Lake One meadows by fringes of willow bush and black spruce. Aspen-covered sand ridges, grading into black-spruce/feather-moss communities bordered the area to the north. The wolves used the site frequently and it became crisscrossed with numerous trails connecting activity sites, beds, and play-dens.

A second rendezvous site was first occupied in the second week of July. It came into existence by a gradual extension of movements from the first site. The pups extended their movements in various directions from the first site as they followed adults or met them upon their return from hunting forays, and it seems they gradually occupied the new location, which became the focal point of their activities. The second rendezvous site was situated on the slope of a low, sandy ridge close to an abandoned nursery den used two years earlier. The site had signs of former battles—remains of a young bison bull, bones of a beaver, and feathers from a waterfowl.

In mid-July the cow-calf bison herds had largely disappeared from the Lake One meadows. As a possible result the pack extended its hunting forays 4 to 5 kilometers (2.5 to 3.1 miles) northwest to a series of small grassy clearings, low-lying wet areas covered by willow bush, and lower-lying depressions. Here they established a third rendezvous site. Quite close to the site was the carcass of a bull. The cause of death was unknown, but my guess was that it had succumbed to anthrax.

In late August we observed the Lake One pack at a kill. By that time the pack seemed to have abandoned the use of rendezvous sites and was roaming more widely. Soon thereafter we saw two wolf pups alone. They were crying out in mournful howls and searching about erratically. All signs suggested they had been abandoned by the pack. The ultimate fate of these two animals we never knew, but it is quite possible it was less than happy. Whether they were inadvertently or deliberately abandoned was not clear.

Our tower observations at Lake One included unique opportunities to study the interactions of bison and wolves in close proximity to each other. All 166 wolf/bison encounters we observed here during the summer of 1980 were analyzed to learn how the hunter and the hunted cope with each other. Admittedly, human observers can interpret what they see only from the limited faculties and senses available to them. Invariably, the interpretations are colored by those limitations. Regardless, the Lake One insights opened for us windows on the world of the delta bison and the wolves that prey on them.

That each needs the other is true, though perhaps not immediately evident. Clearly, wolves depend on bison as food; how bison depend on wolves is less obvious. Without wolves present, and in the absence of hunting by humans, bison numbers would increase, likely even in the presence of diseases, to the point where they would destroy their own food supply. The killing of bison by wolves serves to reduce the numbers, thereby reducing bison density and likely raising overall health of the bison population as a whole. Native elders have told me that they believe "if you leave the buffalo alone, they will cure themselves." Evolution as seen by the northerners. And, of course, the weak bison, the diseased, are probably at a disadvantage and make for easier prey. But killing is not restricted to the disadvantaged. Wolves will kill healthy animals if the opportunity arises.

Tim and I studied the wolves as they watched, trailed, pursued, and attacked the bison, and it was clear to us they were operating as a complex social unit. From our perch Tim and I felt we were beginning to understand what a wolf might do next. We never felt we could always predict the next move, but through careful observations of many packs and various individuals over the years we began to see the difference between the peculiarities of an individual and the more universal, species-specific traits. We were cautious about reaching conclusions regarding general wolf behavior because so much of what we observed was colored by individual personalities.

One pattern we began to see was that wolves travel either together in hunting units or as single animals. Single wolves may be lone wolves but are more likely wolves who belong to a pack and who, at the time of observation, happen to be traveling without companions. Lone wolves do not belong to packs. Retired Alpha Male was an oddity. I considered him an independent wolf that was not incorporated into the pack but had access to it and could come and go as he pleased. Perhaps he was indeed a fourth type of wolf, neither lone wolf nor fully integrated pack member, or perhaps the social structure of wolves is far more complicated than we suspect.

When Tim and I worked at Lake One, we recorded twice as many wolf-bison encounters involving packs than single wolves. Wolves display a range of interest from ignoring the herd, to merely watching, to attacking. Comparing single and pack wolves revealed some notable differences. Single wolves spent a greater proportion of their time merely watching bison as compared to wolves in packs; as pack animals individuals were more likely to test the vulnerability of a herd or single bison. Pack wolves were three times as likely to "approach" a herd—a behavior that initially has the appearance of an attack but does not result in an actual attack. Of the ten times we saw wolves make physical contact with bison, ten times in two years, only one involved a single wolf. To us, the advantages of pack life seemed clear.

When wolf packs attacked, they definitely showed a

preference for herds with calves; single wolves were almost seven times more likely than packs to test bull-only herds. That seemed odd until we looked at the definition of "testing." In reality it was likely a function of a search image in packs—going after cow-calf herds, while the single wolves were more prone to chance encounters with bison, including the more scattered bull herds. When the single wolves bumped into a group of bulls, they checked it out. The packs moved on. Single wolves never were great buffalo hunters. Hunting alone they scrounged for food, chasing down muskrat or waterfowl and along the way encountering the small isolated bull herds. A trapper once told me that one winter he tracked a lone wolf to a kill site of an old bison bull. He did not know what condition the old bull was in when it was killed by the wolf.

Bison do not just wait around to be harassed and killed. They can put up spirited defenses when necessary. Tim and I recorded one of the most sustained and successful bison defenses against predation we ever witnessed. It involved an unusual grouping of a single cow, her calf, and a herd of fifteen bulls. It lasted throughout an entire day. The wolves were relentless, being turned away but always coming back for more. The bulls were determined to help this damsel in distress. During several of the attacks the bison group became fragmented, resulting in a momentary isolation of cow with calf, but the bison managed to regroup before the kill could be made. The young bulls were particularly effective in protecting the calves.

The battle began at 6:20 on a May morning. The herd was resting; four wolves were close by, lying down at a distance of 200 paces. The wolves made no effort to conceal themselves, but didn't seem ready to take on the bulls. Eventually the bulls started to feed, and at 7:20 A.M. they gradually began dispersing as they grazed. The cow led her calf away from the wolves and soon began running. The wolves followed. The cow took her calf into the relative safety of an area occupied by five of the bulls. The wolves pressed the attack, with one heading straight for the calf. Its mother wheeled about and charged the wolf with head low and tail raised. The other three wolves then slipped past the cow and went for the calf. In a moment the five bulls had rushed to the calf's rescue and surrounded it. They pointed their sharp horns outward, forming a protective line. There was little the wolves could do to the calf, protected as it was by this armada. The wolves retreated. The cow positioned herself next to the calf, and surrounded by bulls, mother and young walked to higher ground. The wolves followed.

As the herd moved on, it tended to spread out, the bulls getting feisty and butting one another. A lone bull that had become separated from the herd charged Female Helper and Alpha Male causing the former to retreat and the latter to move well to the side. Tagalong Male then met up with Female Helper and both joined Alpha Male. Alpha Female lagged behind. Again the herd bunched up to surround the cow and calf, most watching the wolves, which were 200 paces to the northeast. All four wolves then lay down in a lowland sedge area, but they kept their heads up and seemed alert. At 8:35 A.M. the bison again gradually spread out to graze, and the cow and her offspring were no longer surrounded by the ring of bulls. Female Helper rose, trotted to the southwest, and initiated a new attack. At first the bulls seemed to ignore the cow. Then four wolves flashed by the bulls in pursuit of the calf. Alpha Male caught up first and was turned aside by the charging cow. He veered around and soon caught up to his mates who were in pursuit of the running calf. In a moment the calf was in the grasp of the wolves. They pulled it down to the ground. The calf managed to quickly struggle free and ran off in a semicircle toward its mother. The cow rejoined the calf and at the same moment they were joined by the bulls. Bull after bull charged the circling wolves with horns forward and tails raised. The cow stood with her head turned aside; the calf was pressed against her flank.

Female Helper and Alpha Male trotted 150 paces east of the bison herd. Tagalong Male and Alpha Female patrolled the opposite side of the herd. Shortly, the cow raised her tail and trotted off, leading the calf and the bulls southward. As they moved on, the bulls charged Alpha Male and Female Helper, who were quickly forced back. The other wolves followed and were rewarded with an opportunity when the calf and its mother fell behind the moving bulls. The wolves moved quickly to take advantage of what looked like a chance to make a kill. The cow turned to meet them as her calf ran to the bulls. The bulls, sensing that danger threatened the cow and calf, crowded in again, advancing toward the wolves.

Fifteen minutes later, three bulls, the cow, and her calf came into proximity of the larger herd. Other bulls were grazing and lying down chewing their cud. The wolves rested 100 paces north of the herd. At 9:10 A.M., three hours after the attack had begun, Female Helper rose and cautiously moved among the herd. Alpha Male and Tagalong Male followed. When all three were near the bulls, the cow, the calf, and their three bull escorts peeled away from the larger herd. The wolves trotted behind but again retreated when the bulls turned on them. Seven other bulls approached from the north and chased the wolves aside.

At 9:15 A.M. the cow and calf, with a five-bull escort, walked farther southwest close to cover. The remaining bulls had lagged behind, grazing in widely scattered groups. Female Helper trotted first south, then east until well past the cow-calf group. Alpha Male and Tagalong Male walked among the trailing bulls while Alpha Female sat and watched from the north. At first it seemed that the wolves wanted to prevent the cow and calf from entering the bush, but it soon became obvious that they were trying to stampede and scatter the small herd composed of the cow, her calf, and the escorting bulls. It worked. The cow and calf broke away from the bulls and headed for the protection of the bush. Female Helper raced with Alpha Male and Tagalong Male to cut them off before they could disappear into the bushes. The cow and calf then veered back to join the closest bulls.

Meanwhile, Alpha Female wandered into the bush and out of sight. The cow and calf had re-formed a small herd with the bulls but it was ephemeral. The wolves were working the situation to their advantage, and soon the bulls were in the bush with the calf and cow left behind in the open. The cow, instead of fleeing with the bulls, headed southeast, then turned abruptly along the side of a sand ridge to join another group of several bulls. It seemed like a good move; the wolves were kept at bay. The new protectors and the cow grazed for a bit. After wandering back and forth along the ridge for a time, the four wolves lay down about 30 paces from the shielded calf. Eventually, the cow descended the ridge and headed north at a fast walk. The calf, however, stayed with the bulls and soon its mother was 150 paces away. Then the calf darted after its mother. As soon as the calf descended the ridge, Alpha Male apparently saw an opportunity and all four wolves immediately advanced from the south. The cow quickly ran back and escorted her calf up the ridge while the wolves were intercepted at the top of the ridge by several young bulls.

By 9:40 A.M. all four wolves had retreated to a spruce and willow swamp southwest of the ridge. Alpha Male remained in the open. Soon, the cow headed north off the ridge and across the meadow in what appeared to be her third attempt to lead the calf away from the wolves. After proceeding 400 paces, she stopped and turned to wait for her reluctant calf to follow. The calf started to make a move. When it was 50 paces from the ridge, Alpha Male came around the ridge to begin the fourth attack. Starting from a halting gait, the wolf immediately leveled into a fast lope on the calf's heels. The calf quickly caught up to its mother and both ran northward. After 600 paces of close pursuit, the cow turned to defend her calf. The calf swung around and was knocked down by Alpha Male who had deftly dodged the cow. The calf scrambled to its feet and fled with a burst of speed toward the ridge and an approaching young bull. The wolf tried to stay with the calf but suddenly found himself intercepted by the cow who struck him hard with her forefeet. Alpha Male rolled over once, came to his feet, raced quickly around the young bull, and almost caught the calf as it ascended the ridge. At the same time three other wolves came leaping over the ridge only to find the calf suddenly surrounded by three bulls. The cow returned in seconds to help drive off the excited wolves.

At 10:00 A.M. the bison descended the ridge, moving slowly southeast. Alpha Male, Tagalong Male, and Alpha Female had retreated to a small aspen stand bordering the meadow's southern reach, but Female Helper trotted off behind the herd. She rushed the calf but was thwarted by charging bulls. The bulls were quick to resume normal activity but the cow and calf remained highly alert. At 10:30 the cow headed east, the calf again lagging behind with three young bulls. The wolves, standing at the edge of the trees, proceeded into the meadow when the calf and a young bull started trailing after the cow. When the calf drew ahead of the bull, Alpha Male launched into a halting gait, his three followers close behind. The wolves were about 300 paces behind when the cow and the bull spun around to defend the calf. Wolves flowed around them and avoided their charges. The cow bolted northeast with her calf as three more bulls approached from the ridge. But the bulls were outmaneuvered by the wolves. Alpha Male grabbed the back of the calf's left flank only to be chased off by two bulls and the cow. A skirmish ensued, bulls charging, wolves dodging and rushing the calf, the calf trying to keep close to its mother's side. Two of the wolves grabbed the calf and brought it to the ground. It squirmed, got up, and took off running. Three wolves pulled the calf down again but the adult bison chased them off. All four wolves were now very excited, prancing around, circling and darting, looking for an opening as bulls and cows shielded the calf. Alpha Male persisted, finally grabbing the calf for the eighth time. But he was chased off again by the cow.

The calf was wounded in several places and began to move more slowly. When it stood, it wobbled. The cow took the calf northeast, trotting, four younger and two mature bulls following the cow. The wolves were visibly tired but persisted. Alpha Male kept up the pace. When the herd stopped and gathered near an aspen bluff, the wolves retired to tall grass and rested.

Soon, the cow moved off again with her calf, followed by two bulls. The wolves immediately sprang up and gave chase. When they overtook the foursome, the two bulls wheeled to charge, but the wolves bypassed them and quickly overtook the fleeing cow and calf. The cow also turned on them but they veered around her and caught up with the still-running calf. Two wolves grabbed the calf by the hind legs but it kicked itself free as it ran. Three nearby bulls rushed in to protect it. Alpha Male, always the most persistent, charged the group but was forced to retreat. The pack circled around the bison looking for an opening. When the remainder of the bulls caught up, the herd formed a tight formation and started to walk back in a northeasterly direction.

At 11:05 A.M. the cow and calf suddenly ran eastward again, with the bulls trotting 20 paces behind. Alpha Male and Female Helper sprinted after them, the former pulling ahead with Tagalong Male and Alpha Female trailing. The cow turned and ran back to the bulls who shielded the calf. Again she bolted, heading northwest with her calf. The waiting wolves rushed in, but not soon enough; four young bulls closed around the twosome. Again the cow ran off, her calf and one bull trailing. The wolves were panting hard and appeared to be tiring, but they still gave chase. Alpha Female was trailing. A standoff developed, with the cow and one bull protecting the calf. Then the bull charged, allowing Female Helper and Alpha Male to lunge at the calf. The calf wheeled around the cow, who also charged the wolves. The youngster struck a wider circle to join three bulls. Before it could escape, Alpha Male and Tagalong Male grabbed the calf by the rump and dragged it to the ground. The cow and bulls chased them off as the calf scrambled to its feet and ran back to the ridge followed by two young bulls and the cow. Once more the pack nearly caught up to the calf, but the bulls were surprisingly fast and the wolves failed to reach their prey.

Five hours had now elapsed since the chase began. The wolves continued their attacks and the calf continued to survive the ordeal. But the young buffalo showed signs of injury and was bleeding from various small cuts. At 11:10 the wolves launched another ten-minute attack. As the herd walked quickly along, Alpha Male, Tagalong Male, and Female Helper ran up alongside, darting in and out, trying to reach the unfortunate calf. Harassed, the herd turned back toward aspen cover. They walked briskly, with a young bull out front. With Alpha Male in the lead, the wolves followed; they were panting and appeared to be exhausted. The cow waited a moment for the other bulls to join the group, then continued on. The wolves lagged behind. Only Alpha Male accelerated his pace when the cow and calf outdistanced the rest of the herd, but now even he was unable to overtake them. The wolves initiated rushes from time to time. Although the calf walked stiffly, limping on at least one leg, it could still run and seemed to have sufficient stamina when needed. The herd grazed for an hour and then drank water.

By 1:30 in the afternoon everyone was resting. They stayed down until 4:30 P.M. Finally, the cow and calf got up, the calf managing to do so only slowly. The herd had now gotten closer to the tower, and Tim could see bloodstained wounds on the upper left front leg where it joined the chest, on the forehead, and along the lower hind legs. The upper right hind leg was noticeably swollen. There was no sign of active, profuse bleeding.

Fifteen minutes after the calf arose, Alpha Male appeared from the north, trotting in an almost straight line toward it. Three other wolves followed at a distance. Alpha Male bypassed the older bulls, who ignored him, but he was then discovered by the larger cow-calf herd. The bison drew together and walked to higher ground; the wolves seemed resigned to defeat. Alpha Male rejoined the other pack members. They were already 600 paces from the herd when, for some unknown reason, the cow seemed to get nervous and bolted. She led her calf away from the herd's protection. Alpha Male looked back and saw them. Immediately, he started back, breaking into a fast lope through hummocky, water-soaked turf. The wolf soon overtook and bypassed the cow, but the calf, out in front, reached a single bull who swung around defiantly. As the calf fled to the bull's side, Alpha Male, unable to stop and perhaps intending to ambush the calf, appeared to leap over the bull's rump. Matters developed so quickly that "leap" is simply our interpretation of what occurred. Now cow and bull, with backs arched and tails raised, shielded the calf from the prancing, excited wolf. Exhausted, the wolves relented.

At 5:30 the wolves were back. The cow, calf, and one mature bull were grazing only fifty paces from Female Helper. This subordinate female kept up a brisk, steady pace as if ignoring the bison, then suddenly rushed the calf. The bull spotted her and charged. The cow reached her calf and Female Helper was forced to retreat. At 6:00 Alpha Male entered the meadow, exactly where Female Helper had earlier appeared, and trotted northwest. Despite the high visibility of his white fur, the wolf was very close to the calf before the adults seemed to take notice. The cow rushed up to face Alpha Male, but the wolf outmaneuvered her and raced after the calf. It ran in a tight circle trying to shake off the predator and return to safety but was attacked for the eleventh time and bitten on the right shoulder. The cow and bull chased Alpha Male off. From ten paces away he continued to circle the huddled trio, tail wagging, then he suddenly abandoned the attempt.

This was the last encounter. From the tower Tim

watched the bison drift out of sight as night fell. The next morning the wolves had left and the calf was still with its mother. The herd of bulls was seen frolicking about as if nothing had happened the day before.

A day later, early in the morning, a herd of fifty-five cows, calves, yearlings, and bulls moved by our camp. We could not tell whether the heroic calf had joined them, but it was hard not to hope so. Individuals shuffled along, grazing in a loose formation, and large fluffs of winter coat-remains dangled from the sides and necks of older cows. A complement of blackbirds, starlings, and cowbirds fluttered around the trailing animals, using the bison as perches from which to hunt for food. Two male cowbirds put on a courtship display upon the back of a bull, hoping to entice a female. The low morning sun caught the iridescence of reflected light as the males fluffed their wings and puffed up their feathers. Bison appeared hallowed in gold against the backlight; in the distance only elongated wisps of mist remained. The air was filled with the constant din of cows grunting, almost piglike, maintaining a verbal link with the six calves ready to spend their first summer on the lush green sedge meadows.

Reflecting on the relentless wolf attacks, it is clear that the calf survived initially because of its incredible speed and agile recovery when downed. Ultimately, however, without the constant intervention by the bulls, the calf would have been doomed. The younger bulls were particularly effective. In all my years in Wood Buffalo, I never again encountered such a tenacious defense by bison of any age group or sex. Was it an unusual occurrence? Or does it happen often when there are no human eyes to observe it?

Recalling events witnessed from the perch is only possible because we kept detailed field diaries. Below is a composite of our observations of wolf encounters with a mixed herd of about thirty-four bison that began the summer with six calves. Alpha Male and his pack preyed on this cow-calf herd, providing an interesting contrast to the cow and calf that sought the company of the bulls. The events are reported chronologically.

June 6, 1980: The [above] herd [at the time consisting of twenty-one cows, six calves, four yearlings, and three unclassified animals] was observed from 2:40 to 5:00 P.M. The herd was seen resting at the edge of a bush and was under constant surveillance by four wolves. Bison intermittently stood up, were seen briefly grazing or nursing calves. There were no major movements until 4:00 P.M. Wolves did not relax their vigilance throughout. At 9:30 P.M. this herd was seen, again moving restlessly. Calves, whether resting or moving, appeared to favor the midarea of the herd. Wolves followed the moving herd in an uncoordinated fashion.

June 12, 1980: At 6:35 A.M. the herd moved along the edge of Lake One meadow while Female Helper was trailing the herd at 50 to 250 paces. The wolf veered around the herd and entered a shrubby area while the bison began to graze. Cows with calves moved in the central portion of the herd. Bison moved into cover and were followed by two wolves. At 7:30 the herd stampeded out of the bush, several rear adults turning, as if facing wolves, which were not visible. Then the herd returned into the bush along a migration trail. At least two wolves followed and, although not witnessed (dense vegetation), a calf was attacked and killed. Chase in the bush was for about 300 paces. A cow was seen at 1:30 P.M. moving about quickly, suggesting stress. Vocalization included grunting. The cow charged Alpha Male while he was feeding on the calf. The cow returned to her calf two more times that day (7:20 and 10:00 P.M.). It was noticed that the cow had received gashes along the upper left flank and that her tail was missing. Portions of the tail were found at the kill site. Virtually nothing remained of the calf carcass within a few hours. Left were small tufts of hair, small portions of both scapula, a small portion of the pelvis, and a portion of the lower jaw. Losing tails to wolves is a common occurrence in the park.

June 13, 1980: Another calf within the same herd was seen limping; it was walking slowly and had trouble getting up to its feet.

June 14, 1980: Only four calves were seen, therefore, two were missing, of which one was unaccounted for. Observations of the curious behavior of one cow (identical to that observed in the cow that had lost her calf on the twelfth of June) and the persistent movement of Alpha Male to a specific area also frequented by the cow was strong evidence that the

limping calf had been killed and consumed by
wolves.

June 15, 1980: At 10:20 P.M. two wolves (Female Helper
and Alpha Female) were seen feeding on a bison calf
while Alpha Male rested nearby. Inspection of the kill
an hour later revealed that mortal wounds were
inflicted to the right shoulder, exposing the lungs.
Flesh from the left femur was all that had been consumed. Rigor mortis had not set in and it is likely
that the calf had been chased and killed in an open
meadow. Trampled grass for 20 paces indicated the
trail of attack. Examination of the site one day later
revealed that all portions were either eaten or had
been dragged away, as the only evidence of the kill
was trampled and bloodstained grass.

To limit our account of observations from the perch at
Lake One only to kills would be misleading. Although our
observations were focused on the strategy of wolf attacks
and prey survival, we also witnessed the birth of calves. I
once saw a cow eating the afterbirth while the newly born
calf was still wet and in need of maternal attention. I have
never seen afterbirth protruding from a cow hours after the
birth of a calf as described in captive bison. The afterbirth
contains hormones, apparently sufficiently potent to arouse
intense interest by young bulls. Cows immediately consumed the afterbirth in our study, probably for a number
of reasons, such as reducing aggression by bulls and not
attracting predators.

Tim first saw a calf being born on May 12, 1980.
Following the birth, the cow exhibited curious antagonis-

A cow defending her dead calf, which was killed by the pack in early morning

tic behavior toward the youngster. Repeatedly, she interrupted nursing sessions with such violent bouts of butting and pushing the newborn to the ground that nearby bulls were attracted to the scene. The cow and her calf soon disappeared into the bushes so we never knew how this episode ended. Tim witnessed another birth on June 3. The cow was part of a mixed herd of ninety-one bison, and three wolves were watching them from the perimeter. The birth took place between 5:35 and 7:30 A.M. He first saw the calf at 7:35 A.M., still wet; the afterbirth was still protruding from the cow. Apparently the cow did not leave the herd and parturition took place at the edge of a meadow adjacent to an island of bush. Soon after birth the newborn was attacked by wolves. The cow led the calf, still wobbly on its legs, to the safety of the herd center. Even though the wolves must have smelled the newborn, they did not persist in the attack. The calf in turn quickly developed its motor skills and within a very short time (minutes) could keep up with the moving herd. The bond between mother and calf is very strong. I have seen yearlings still trying to nurse. Heifers, or female calves, retain the bond with mothers longer then male calves. Weaning for some bull calves occurs in October, about six months after birth. What determined weaning schedules was never clear to me.

Young calves spend a great deal of time in social groups, which I call pods. I thought long and hard about what to call these "kindergarten" groups of youngsters and came up with this designation, which traditionally is applied to whales. It seemed to me that in open delta spaces, as in oceans, youngsters that stick together are not confined to structures. Pods seemed to be a good designation for such groups. In early May newborn calves stay with their mothers. Pod formation is most noticeable from about the third week of May to about the third week of July. Because the herds largely disappear from the Lake One area in August, we could not establish whether pod formation continued at this time; by the end of August, when mixed herds had returned to Lake One, pod formation was reduced but not absent.

Calves can be seen any time of the year within Wood Buffalo National Park. This is unusual among hoofed animals, most of whom bear young only in the spring. For example, the peak time of calf production for bottle-fed bison raised in pens in the small native community of Fort Resolution is April 22 to June 10 each year. These animals are captured from wild herds that are found at roughly the same latitude each time. The earliest calf was born there on March 25 and the latest on October 7. (The biologist John Nishi kindly provided this information.) This means that some anomaly must be operating within Wood Buffalo National Park. The presence of diseases could be a cause of asynchronous calving periods.

Living with the Lake One wolf pack was an incredible experience. We followed, we watched, and we recorded what we saw as the wolves went about their normal activities. The open spaces of the Lake One meadows allowed us to see long distances, and we followed the herds in order to be with the wolves. In time the wolves accepted us as part of the landscape, much as the Jasper wolves had done. But we never intentionally habituated the animals as I had done in Jasper National Park. Also, unlike in earlier studies, I was not alone. Together Tim and I observed the wolves. Initially just "wild dogs" differentiated only by the color of their coats, the wolves became individuals as we learned more about them, thus taking on distinct personalities. This kind of information is rarely the substance of modern biological investigations. And cold hard statistics cannot convey the intricacies of natural processes; they leave out the fine-scaled details that can only be obtained through close observation.

The time Tim and I spent at the tower also taught us something about how wolves and bison live with one another. Only rarely are wolves not in proximity of a bison herd, though they are not always with the same herd. A pack may leave the herd and travel long distances, but it always returns to the same general vicinity. Meanwhile the

A single wolf returning from a hunt walks by a resting herd.

original herd may have moved on, to be picked up by another pack, and a new herd will have taken its place. Curiously, bison will tolerate wolves in their midst for hours at a time. As if they have not a care in the world, they lie down, chew the cud, and nurse or groom the calves while older youngsters playfully chase one another, running in circles, butting, and mounting like adult bulls. At times the scene is surrealistic, like the Garden of Eden. Yet, always, the peace treaty is only temporary, and soon Eden becomes Gallipoli.

An Eagle's-Eye View

By the late 1970s I had gained a good deal of experience working with wolves, tracking them in winter and habituating them in summer. I was not familiar with aerial darting of wolves from a helicopter, but I needed to apply this method to the open landscapes of Wood Buffalo National Park. Enter a promising graduate student named Sebastian Oosenbrug and the help of biologists from the Northwest Territories. Because of the immensity of the study area, we decided to concentrate most of our aerial work north of the Peace River, and Sebastian made his headquarters in the town of Fort Smith.

Bison in a winter landscape from 500 meters (1,640 feet) above sometimes resemble a column of soldiers on the

A bison herd in midwinter. Winter foraging involves opening up snow craters to access the cured sedges and grasses underneath.

move. Airborne, I had the advantage of the field marshal watching troops from a hillside, seeing strategies invisible from the ground. I had been a foot soldier among the herds and the spy in the tower; now I could see it all from the air. Each viewpoint had its advantages and disadvantages.

One of Sebastian's first challenges for collaring wolves was to capture them. Trapping was a possibility, but because of the inaccessibility of many sites it was less practical than aerial darting. Techniques for aerial darting of wolves had been used in northern Canada so we knew the basics. Now we had to apply them. A fixed-wing plane was used to find the wolves, scanning a large region looking for wolf packs in open areas. Once the wolves were located, the helicopter sprang into action. The capture team in the helicopter consisted of a pilot, one shooter, and two observers. The spotter plane would circle high over the open meadows and direct them to the location of the pack.

After a specific target wolf was selected, the helicopter would swoop down and position itself behind and close to the running wolf. It was up to the shooter to do the rest. There was a sense of excitement and adventure to the undertaking. The first time I was the shooter, I leaned out of the helicopter and felt the adrenaline course through my system as I tried to aim carefully at a moving target while sitting in a hopelessly unstable perch about 20 meters (65 feet) behind the animal. The helicopter propellers created a windstorm that added to the difficulties of trying to be a proficient marksman. Surprise is the only word to describe

An aerial view of wolves at Lousy Creek meadows. The largest pack size seen in the fall numbered more than thirty individuals at one rendezvous site.

the thrill I felt when my first shot was a perfect score. I could see the colored dart hit the rump of the wolf, stick in place, and quickly take effect. As luck (and some skill) would have it, all the wolves we darted (forty-three of them) were unharmed. A poorly placed shot could have penetrated vital organs in the chest, stomach, or head.

Once the capture team landed the drugged wolves were weighed, measured, ear-tagged, and collared with radio transmitters. After recovering from the drugs, the wolves rejoined their packs. We called these animals the "Judas wolves," the spies within the pack. As long as the collar of a Judas wolf was functional and the animal stayed with the pack, the private lives of that individual pack would be available to the prying eyes of the biologist conducting the monitoring overhead from an airplane. That meant daily or weekly flights to relocate the animals. Sebastian carefully juggled the schedule to keep track of all the wolves.

Each contact with a wolf was mapped, providing us with an outline of the territory used by that pack. However, the "eagle's-eye" perspective allowed for gathering even more data. We watched packs trying to kill bison and, rarely, moose; measured the length of time they surrounded a beleaguered herd; saw how they "strategized" the attacks; recorded which wolves did most of the damage to the intended victims; and determined the length of chases, kill rates, food consumption, and scavenging by other wildlife species and the behavior of pack wolves toward individual members in a pack—or between packs. Answers to the questions were often incomplete, but with time more pieces of the puzzle came into focus. The task for Sebastian was to monitor collared packs, daily if possible. Each morning, he and his assistants would climb into his small plane and taxi out on a frozen runway to take to the skies. I joined him when I could. From the air, bison and wolves look like ants on the snow, small dark spots on a blanket of white. Yet a trained observer can easily distinguish the difference between bison tracks and wolf tracks. Wolves, hence their tracks, wander more when the snow is not too deep. From the air it is possible to see a pattern of braided footprints, meaning wolves do not follow in each other's footsteps. This allows the observer to count the number of individuals traveling together in a pack. In deep snow, on the other hand, wolves, like bison, follow single file, making traveling much easier. Even then it is easy to distinguish wolf tracks from bison tracks. The viewer gets his clues from the pattern of travel. Occasionally from an aerial view other behavioral information can be collected. A wolf may leave the main trail to begin digging out an old den. At other times, tracks may lead to a clump of grass or a tree stump where a dominant wolf will leave his scent. Bison trails are more direct and invariably end up in feeding craters.

During winter, bison left to their own activity rhythms appear to be quite sedentary. Resting and foraging occupy much of their time. I cannot recall ever having seen herds moving around in winter on a sustained basis; I never got the impression the animals were in a rush to get somewhere. Herds seek out winter ranges and slowly move around as food availability dictates. That pattern changes in the presence of wolves. Wolves constantly influence herd movements. I came to call wolf packs the "Mix Master" of the Wood Buffalo bison ecosystem. The presence of these predators puts an entirely different complexion into the lives of bison. It is one of many reasons why bison ranching for meat production is unrealistic in wolf country. You either ranch bison and have the potential for profit from meat sales or you establish nature reserves with bison and wolves and sacrifice the profit.

Predators influence bison movements throughout the year, sometimes in concert with the seasonal migrations. In other words, in the presence of wolf predation, the movements of the bison are altered. That is quite different from seasonal movements. In the spring and fall the bison undertake local migrations. As an example, the third week of May was always the best time to see bison heading south to areas along Lousy and Lynx Stand Creeks. Within that predictable migration, wolves might influence the pattern of the movements.

Snow depths are critical. Heavy, deep snow, particularly if it forms crusts, hinders the bison in their foraging, and it takes extra energy to travel through the snow. An adult bull can weigh more than 900 kilograms (almost 2,000 pounds) and a cow somewhat less; it appears almost miraculous that such large animals can find enough food to survive when the snow can attain depths of up to 100 centimeters (39 inches). Bison dig through the snow by pawing and swinging their heads back and forth, opening craters. A bison uses its head like a snow shovel, swinging it back and forth at a rate of about five to seven times per minute. Head swings are accomplished by pushing the muzzle into the snow surface followed by back and forth movement of the massive head, clearing away snow and forming a crater. The animal then feeds on the exposed vegetation, steps forward, and repeats the procedure. The active feeding zone proceeds from the edge of a group crater, where the undisturbed snow is constantly being opened up in search of food. The use of the head as a snow-clearing organ is facilitated by the strong neck muscles and the musculature of the hump. Facial hair helps protect the skin from abrasion. Winter feeding behavior also includes pawing, nose pushing, and chin pulling. Pawing is a downward and backward movement of a raised front leg and is often used to break crust on the snow's surface. A nose push is a forward thrust displacing the snow with the muzzle; a chin pull is a backward motion pulling the head toward the body. Hard as it is to find food under the snow, midwinter warm spells make matters worse. The surface layers melt, then, when temperatures drop, freeze anew, forming a firm crust that makes it harder for the bison to access food.

Individual feeding craters are formed, which eventually become connected to form group craters. An elaborate trail system connects group craters used for feeding areas. Group craters are also where most of the social interactions of bison take place in winter. They are the places where bison rest and ruminate and where calves engage in playful activities. Wolves, too, spend much of their leisure time resting at these craters. Areas disturbed by bison become hard and are easy to walk on, reducing the energy normally required to move around. Yet energy is expended in great quantities when wolves attack and chase the bison into deep snow zones.

Flying over the landscape in winter was like opening up a new chapter of a book and reading about the lives of wolves and bison when ice and snow have a grip on the landscape. Winter gives predator and prey much wider access to the different habitats. Bison can seek out new foraging sites and not be restricted to areas with solid footing. It was exciting to view the movement and grazing patterns of the bison herds from the air. But the snow cover had more to reveal.

Gripping, often brutal, stories are told by the tracks and other evidence left behind after a predation event. The trampling of wolf feet and bison hooves are intertwined as evidence of struggles between the two. When the wolves win (a regular outcome), one sees long bones, bits of hides, skull caps with the horns of the victim, resting beds of wolves, and black, blood-splattered streaks of liquid droppings that biologists call "blood scat." The blood scat, which results from the first meal after a kill, a feast of organs and blood-rich tissue, is black and in a liquid form.

One early February day, Sebastian and I took to the sky to monitor a pack of eight wolves. In early February the pack had been chasing a herd of ninety bison. After several attempts the pack discontinued their attacks. However, when we returned the next day, we could tell from the tracks in the snow that the pack had not given up. They had been relentless in their pursuit of a victim. Not until a week later had the pack killed a cow from that herd. The final chase was a short one. Yet the herd had run for another 20 kilometers (12 miles) before we saw evidence of its stopping to rest. Even more dramatic events were yet to come.

Thinking back over the events we had recorded, Sebastian and I decided that the wolves in this pack must have gone without food for some time, possibly several days. We didn't know with any degree of certainty whether the pack had been successful at another location in the interim. Since we were using conventional radio-tracking equipment, we obtained fixed locations at intervals, thus we could not put together a continuous record. Today we could. Ecology has developed in concert with technology, and just as I have studied from the ground, the loft, and the sky, a modern approach would now involve satellite tracking, giving virtually continuous records of movement. The satellite locates the wolves; the computer plots the locations; and the biologist analyzes the data. But the new technology eliminates some dimensions of scientific inquiry: no one observes the bloody kill or measures qualitative information acquired at the scene.

We lost contact with that pack for awhile, but by March 6 the herd and the same pack were seen together again—once more in a "crisis mode." Snow conditions were excellent. The story left in the snow told us that the herd had not been cratering. Instead, the herd was in a tight formation, bunched together on compacted and solidly trampled snow. This scenario lasted until March 8 when the wolves were seen resting close to the herd and the bison were standing with "resigned" postures, not feeding, facing the wolves. It is likely that constant testing through persistent attacks by the wolves occurred in our absence. Something had to give—either the wolves would relent and search for a new herd or the bison would be forced to run, in which case the wolves had a better chance to isolate a victim.

That night, or early in the morning before we arrived, the pack connected. At 10:45 A.M. we flew over the area and saw the pack resting near a kill. We had to reconstruct events by doing some backtracking from the air. On retracing the chase, we were able to see it had gone on for a 4-kilometer (2.5-mile) stretch in open meadows. Then the advantage turned in favor of the wolves. The chase led into a forest-covered terrain. Once the herd was in forest cover, a calf had been killed within two hundred paces from the wooded edge. In this instance, it appeared that the trees had acted like a net, holding the calf back as the adults crashed through the vegetation in a headlong attempt to flee from the enemy. Isolated from the herd the calf likely stood no chance of escape. Once the kill was made the pack began to feed on the carcass. The herd continued running for 20 kilometers (12 miles) through the bush, came to a plowed road, and ran for another 62 kilometers (38.5 miles) before stopping. One could clearly read the "record" from the air. Tracks "together" meant an all-out running; tracks "braided" meant a less intense chase; the "presence of dung" meant the herd had rested; and "cratering in the snow" meant feeding. In this case the herd had not been able to feed for at least twelve hours (more likely not substantially for about sixty-five hours). In that time the herd had traveled a distance of 86 kilometers (53 miles). The exceptional stamina of these large, hoofed mammals is remarkable.

Chris Vogt's observations tell another story about bison stamina. Chris is a grader operator who, for more than twenty years, patrolled up and down the roads in Wood Buffalo National Park. Two wolves, he once told me, "killed three bison in a twenty-four-hour period." An uncommon occurrence, this happened when wolves were chasing bison along a plowed road where the snow banks were exceptionally high. Once in deep snow the bison were convenient targets. The two wolves had an easy time of it when the bison were completely trapped in the heavy snow cover. He also watched vehicles inadvertently chasing running herds back and forth on plowed roads with steep banks. Bison were reluctant to jump into snow banks to get out of harm's way but sometimes the animals had no other choice. Stamina allowed them to run and run and run, covering long distances.

Much has been debated about the impacts of winter roads on bison ecology. Distances in the north between communities are vast. It is one thing to have winter roads for low-level traffic, another if these roads eventually become high-density transportation corridors. A proposal to upgrade a 118-kilometer (73-mile) trail (right-of-way) came up for public hearings in the winter of 2000. At issue was an intrusion into the park landscape of a road that at low levels of use could be considered a parkway and a means for local people to visit each other to, as one northern resident said, "play poker" and get rid of the winter "blues." When plowed, such roads have pushed bison for up to 160 kilometers (99 miles) at a time—chased first one way then another by vehicles traveling in opposite directions. As Chris Vogt tells the story, "The front ones run because the ones behind push them, and the ones behind cannot look back to see where the danger [wolves/vehicles] is, so the whole herd just keeps going for a long time."

As our flights came to an end, Sebastian had documented 143 chases, kills, and attacks. Of interest was that wolves concentrated most of their efforts on herds rather than smaller groups of bison. It makes sense if one stops to consider that larger herds contain more calves—thus more preferred targets. Also, harrying and testing larger herds meant a greater likelihood of separating that one animal, sometimes though not always a young or weak one, from the group. Offsetting the advantage of hunting the herd is the disadvantage to wolves of the "confusion factor." The confusion factor results from animals in full flight presenting less of a target because the predator cannot zero in on a specific victim. Likely there are offsetting advantages and disadvantages at play. The success rate was much higher for those instances when a pack kept in contact with one herd. Not uncommonly that lasted as long as five to seven days or possibly even longer. The motto for the wolves it seemed was, if at first you don't succeed, try, try again.

Three times during the aerial studies in winter, we observed the killing from beginning to end. On two other occasions we witnessed "near kills," that is the wolves almost had their quarry subdued but the individual managed to rejoin the herd. An example of a bison being separated from a herd and unable to catch up with it again occurred on March 24, 1981, when eight wolves were chasing a herd of twenty-five bison in the northwest corner of the Darough Creek meadows. Sebastian noted the sequence in his journal, and what follows is a reconstruction of his observations.

At 9:40 A.M. the Hornaday River pack was running approximately 1 kilometer [0.6 miles] behind the main portion of a herd of twenty-five bison. The wolves were running in single file over a distance of 500 meters [546 yards], led by one wolf, which was at least 100 meters [109 yards] ahead of the others. Two groups of bison, one of seven and one of two animals, had stopped running and were standing in the line of the chase. At 9:42 the lead wolf reached the second group of bison, after having run past the first group of seven bulls. The two bison (both cows) put their heads down and charged a single wolf as it ran past them. The bison chased the wolf for about ten paces. Two other wolves ran by the two bison, but the remainder of the pack began to harass these two individuals as they reached them by 9:44. As soon as the first three wolves (single and pair) saw that the rest of the pack was attacking the two bison, they ran back and joined in on the attack. We can interpret that as "quick thinking" by the trio. They needed to maximize their chances for success.

By 9:45 A.M. all the wolves were circling, lunging and
snapping at the two cows. One of the cows (lucky
break?) managed to run from the wolves, whereupon
the pack concentrated its attack on the remaining
animal (fate?). Between 9:45 and 9:55, the wolves
were pressing all around the second cow, trying to
get at it from the rear, biting the rump and anal areas.
The cow tried to ward off the attack with its head
but the wolves continued to circle to the rear with
the result that the cow was continually turning in circles. In the meantime this cow tried to rejoin the
herd, which at this point was at least 1 kilometer [0.6
miles] away and still moving into the open meadows.
At 9:55 A.M. the cow, which was visibly tiring as it struggled through the snow with several wolves hanging
onto its hindquarters, moved into a stand of trees.
The harassment and wounding had taken place more
than 750 paces from the first confrontation to where
the cow ended up in trees to face the wolves. By 10:00
both wolves and bison were still in forest cover. The
cow had stopped running but the wolves continued
the attack, coming in from behind and wounding the
cow. Two light-colored wolves were covered with
blood; several wolves were resting as the others continued to press. At 10:05 the victim was standing in
the trees, its hindquarters shaking. As the cow fell
over onto her side, the wolves closed in on her and
immediately began to tear at the abdomen. In a last
desperate attempt to escape, the cow managed to get
up one more time and dragged herself forward for

about 10 more paces, with several wolves holding onto her hindquarters. One would have expected that the animal would have collapsed by now, yet at 10:07 the bison was still on its feet, standing and facing the wolves with its tail up. Some of the wolves were resting nearby and the bison lunged at several standing close; the wolves stepped back. The pattern often repeats itself at this stage. The wolves seemed to recognize that their task of killing could not be undone and there was no longer a need to exert all that extra effort to get the job of killing done.

At 10:15 A.M. the bison was down, head still raised above the ground, as the wolves were again tearing at its abdomen. The wolves were now feeding; the bison's head rose occasionally but it was close to death. The rest of the herd (sixteen animals) had stopped 800 meters [875 yards] to the southeast, at the edge of the open meadow, and some were beginning to graze again.

Each day that we spent in an aircraft looking for a pack we also gathered information on the sizes of packs' territories. Watching packs from ground level one always asks the question "how far does this pack range?" By having a marked animal in each pack and tracking movements from an aircraft, movements and territory sizes can be documented. Packs for which twenty or more available locations were used in the calculations (a defensible sample size), the average territory sizes in winter varied from about 400 square kilometers (154 square miles) to 720 square kilometers (278 square miles) to 1,300 square kilometers (501 square miles) depending on the region of the park and on the method used in calculating territory sizes.

Detailed information from one pack stood out from all the rest in our winter studies. That pack was studied in the area north of the Peace River. It was radio-located many times from the air and over a two-year period used a whopping 3,000 square kilometers of the park (1,158 square miles). We also noted the fluidity with which land tenure was shared by packs. Boundaries changed. We were just getting well started in these studies when the big blow came. The Liberal party lost and the Conservatives took over. Restructuring of the Canadian Wildlife Service had begun.

I had to leave work started undone. I realized that if I was to salvage anything from the research undertaken so far I would have to carry on by myself. Maybe officials thought that "it was time for Carbyn to stop having fun in the bush." Why support given before 1984 should be canceled after 1984 was a complete mystery to all of us in the Canadian Wildlife Service. The explanation given at the time was that there was a "ruling" that our agency did not have a "legal mandate" to carry out this kind of work. The laws had not changed but they were interpreted differently. Certainly, new policy directions are the prerogative of governments and changes in responsibilities are a natural result of such shifts. What is less clear is why research begun by one government should be dropped by another if the work was worthwhile in the first place. The decisions were also haphazardly applied. For example, research on wolves and grizzly bears was discontinued, while that on polar bears was not. By abandoning the Wood Buffalo research efforts, considerable losses accrued to what had already been accomplished. The end result was a major disruption throughout our ranks. I was given new responsibilities as a leader on a swift fox reintroduction project. Some were ready for me to move on to administrative responsibilities, but I was not so sure. Perhaps I was getting older and set in my ways, but I didn't think—maybe *feel* is a better description—that I should abandon Wood Buffalo National Park.

New challenges were interesting and I took them on with great enthusiasm, still every opportunity to get to the park was welcome. One such occasion came unexpectedly. Joel Berger, an imaginative biologist from the University of Nevada called and asked if we could perform an experiment together. It sounded like a great opportunity to once again see the park in winter. Joel's experiment was quite unusual. The question he wanted to test was, are bison still genetically programmed to respond to one of their prehistoric enemies—namely lions? Unlikely as it may sound, lions once roamed across the North American continent. Imagine therefore a landscape with mammoths, mastodons, horses, and camels. After millions of years on the landscape they and their predators—saber-toothed cats, dire wolves, cheetahs, and lions—disappeared some ten thousand to twelve thousand years ago, a blink of an eye in evolutionary terms. Wolves, cougars, and bears are the only large modern predators of any consequence that can kill bison (though coyotes occasionally kill calves). In times past, other large predators also killed bison and the ancestors of bison. It's not something most biologists concern themselves with, but there are exceptions and Joel was one of them. I was eager to go along.

We flew into the park, chartered an airplane, and landed in large meadows near Hay Camp on the north side of the Peace River. Herds of bison were some distance away and we approached them on foot. Loaded with tape recorders, amplifiers, and a host of batteries and cables, we set off on snowshoes and crept up to our quarry. Joel then set up his electronic equipment and broadcast a range of sounds. I, with stopwatch in hand, paid close attention to the reactions of the bison. The idea was that if they were still "genetically wired" to the past, these bison would have it in them to perk up and be alarmed at the roar of a lion. Naturally the expectation is that they would also respond to sounds of their current enemy—the howling of wolves. We had a good chance to test this. You could do that only if you also had a variety of other sounds as controls. That is, to check that it was not just a novel sound that alarmed the bison, we needed to test nonthreatening sounds. I must say it would never have occurred to me to carry out such a test, so I was quite looking forward to the event. I told Joel beforehand that I thought he was not going to get much of a response from wolf howling. On many occasions I have marveled how calm and stoic bison are when, at close range, wolves put on some of their magnificent vocal performances. But Joel had a wider repertoire in mind. He had recordings of howler monkeys, roaring lions, cackling hyenas, red-tailed hawks, chirping crickets, and the rushing sounds of a waterfall. The nonlion and wolf sounds were used as controls. Joel being Joel, the eternal scientist with a vivid imagination and a bent for the unusual, paid little heed to my pessimism. I was glad he did. We need innovative people, and this was surely an unusual and innovative adventure. As I had predicted, responses from our Wood Buffalo bison were not there; they did not have it in them. The odd flicking of an ear, the sideways glance of a bull at a cow's move forward to a neighbor were all I could detect as a response to any of the assorted sounds at varying decibel levels. Joel turned the volume up; lions roared in the sunny winter landscape of the northern bogs—and still no action. Then the howler monkeys! I chuckled to myself at the scope of the undertaking. Well done, Joel, I thought to myself, all in the service of science. These meadows will never hear the like again.

Lousy Creek

I n the 1980s some ecologists were starting to realize that simulation models often had little to do with evaluating the ecology of the animals studied. Models were a useful way to quantify possible relationships but outcomes needed to be tested in the bigger arena. It was still necessary to go out on the vast "stage" provided by nature in order to study nature. Looked at another way, "you cannot be a sailor unless you go out to sea." It was becoming clear to many that the most effective contributions can be made if we think like scientists but not to the exclusion of also being naturalists—or at least some of us, who liked nature, convinced ourselves of this logic to justify our hands-on approach. I knew some things about wolves, because for sixteen years I had followed their trails in western Canada, in Poland, and in Portugal. I had also begun to understand more about the bison of Wood Buffalo National Park. But did I *know* about wolves and bison and their relationship to one another within the northern landscape? I wasn't so sure. After the official studies stopped, it seemed time to get close again by venturing into the open landscape in the southern part of the park.

My first solo trip was in 1985. I scouted an area south of the Peace River. The objective was to follow the herds and obtain counts on calf production and calf survival. From 1986 to 1989 I used the Sweetgrass cabin as my temporary headquarters. Perhaps "headquarters" is too grand a word; it was really just a place where I stored my food and equipment. Initially it was nice to have a base of operation; when things got too rough in the bush, weatherwise, I felt like I was in the lap of luxury if I had a solid roof above my head and a floor under my feet. I would camp in a tent around the area, looking for the herds and coming back to the cabin to get my supplies. Increasingly, I liked the idea of living out of a tent and became less and less dependent on the cabin. I ventured farther afield and moved from the Sweetgrass area farther south into the Lousy Creek area.

By June 1989 I had set up my tent at the forks of Lousy Creek in the hopes of using habituation techniques to get close to the herds and the ever-present packs. My strategy was simple—follow the herds. Wolves are bound to do the same. From beginning to end the creek is about twenty-eight kilometers (seventeen miles) long and serves as a gateway to an extensive portion of the delta that was obviously important to both the wolves and bison. Another creek, Lynx Stand Creek, roughly parallels Lousy Creek and both served as important canoeing routes through my study area. These creeks and their branches extend out as an isthmus into Lake Claire. The general region is known locally as American Point, not to be confused with another nearby site known as Beaver Ass Point.

I had sufficiently mastered the logistics of cooking, eating, and keeping my equipment serviceable so that I was comfortable enough under all weather conditions for longer periods of time without having to store things under a fixed roof. Also, I had long wanted to spend more time along Lousy Creek near what I began to realize was a major bison migration trail. At the forks of Lousy Creek, bison trails led to a large meadow that connected an extension of American Point on Lake Claire to the northern bison wintering areas. Herds congregated here during spring and summer, and signs of wolves denning at various locations were plentiful. On a map the forks are a prominent feature. After walking around the north branch, I discovered though that it was only a remnant of its former watercourse. The northern branch was no more than an overgrown channel with only occasional surface water and marshy vegetation. In the early 1950s Bill Fuller and others traveled this route by motorboat. Now it was a dry channel with a few wet areas.

Bill Fuller was the person who got me interested in Wood Buffalo National Park and also the one who introduced me to Valerius Geist, who greatly influenced my approach to biology. Fuller spent many years as a government biologist in Wood Buffalo into the late 1940s and early 1950s. It was always informative to talk to him about the park and its wildlife. His experiences in the park differed substantially from mine. Bill Fuller was in charge of a selective culling program. Bison were killed in the park for meat production and in an attempt to reduce the incidence of diseases. Much of his data came from carcasses. In later years he became a respected zoologist and served as a member of my graduate program while I was at the University of Alberta. I admired his perspectives on conservation, and his love for the north country was infectious. During subsequent debates regarding the future of bison in Wood Buffalo National Park he took a decidedly different approach from me. Since much of his fieldwork predated mine, and since he had been earlier involved in disease-control work, it was not surprising that our views differed on what to do about diseased herds. His opinion was that they should be destroyed; mine was that you do not destroy a system that has not been studied. I suppose beyond that I really could not see any good biological reasons for implementing and carrying out what many had called the "Armageddon option." People have made too many mistakes through hasty decisions. Unlike many others who shared Fuller's views, Fuller could not be faulted for not having known or worked in the park. He had much experience with the same delta that I have come to know over time.

My first trip on Lousy Creek was in a small rubber raft. The south branch was so shallow, I could only wade in the water, pushing the raft with all my equipment in front of me. The first day in the area was beastly hot and the cool water felt refreshing. But keeping cool was the only advantage of having the raft, because pushing it along was slow and cumbersome. At one point during my first trip with the raft, I had an unusual encounter with wolves. I noticed how first one wolf, then a second wolf, would look my way then disappear, one on each shoreline walking parallel with me through the dense vegetation. The muddied water and profusion of tracks along the banks was a clear sign of the presence of a large bison herd in the area. This was obviously why the wolves were here. They may have wanted to cross, each to the other side, but were prevented from doing so because of my presence in the middle, or possibly they simply wanted to satisfy their curiosity as to what this strange character with the raft was all about. I found this episode entertaining, and who knows, maybe the wolves were similarly entertained by my presence. They never stayed long in the open, merely popping their heads out, then retreating. This went on for a good twenty minutes. Amused, I plodded on pushing the now-cursed raft and, by late in the afternoon, set up camp for my first night at Lousy Creek. I had thought a raft would be an appropriate means of transportation in the shallow waters of a delta. I was wrong and quickly opted for a sixteen-foot canoe that was provided by Scott Flett. Scott was a quiet northern resident, of mixed native and Orkney (European) heritage. He operated the water taxi that took me into and out of civilization for many years.

Lousy Creek was the north country at its best, remaining the focus of my activities for the next eleven years.

A bison herd crossing Lousy Creek

Even its name intrigued me—how did such a wonderful area acquire such an unusual name? The creek was in the heartland of the delta and teeming with wildlife—nothing "lousy" about it. As it turned out, the name may have meant "plentiful." Northern residents use the word "lousy" to imply abundance. The creek was one of the best-known areas for muskrat trapping. People could have been referring to the creek as being "lousy with muskrat" or "lousy with otter" or "lousy with foxes," hence the name Lousy Creek. Another more frequently cited reason for the origin of the name was that families who once camped there had contracted a bad case of body lice and the name "lousy" stuck. A third explanation is that the water is so full of creepy crawly "bugs" that people refer to it as a creek "lousy" with bugs. There will never be an undisputed explanation for the origin of that name. No

LOUSY CREEK STUDY AREA

Map by Andrew D. Raszewski

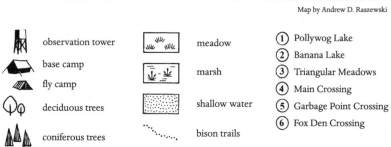

observation tower	meadow	① Pollywog Lake
base camp	marsh	② Banana Lake
fly camp	shallow water	③ Triangular Meadows
deciduous trees	bison trails	④ Main Crossing
coniferous trees		⑤ Garbage Point Crossing
		⑥ Fox Den Crossing

matter; to me, Lousy Creek was nirvana, it could well have been called "God's gift to man" creek.

Judging from the depth of Lynx Stand and the lack of forest cover along its banks (levees), I surmised it must be a much younger watercourse than Lousy Creek. It likely was carved out of the mud flats of the delta deposits. This would occur when water levels drop and standing water needs to find channels to flow into Lake Claire. Another explanation is that these creeks were tributaries of the Peace River that brought in silt deposits to build up the sides. Origins of creeks in the delta have long puzzled me. How some of these stagnant creeks evolved in the first place is a mystery.

Connecting Lynx Stand Creek with Lousy Creek are sedge meadows. I noticed the ephemeral nature of ponds in between. Ephemeral only in recent years, as elders in the Fort Chipewyan community talk of a large lake between the creeks. Older maps and aerial photographs show the outline of lakes. When I first saw the area in 1988, there was a large body of water, which by 1994 had shrunk down to a "puddle." In 1997 it again became a lake and was too deep to walk across. A combination of climate change and the building of a dam upstream may have devastated the wetlands with which I had become familiar. The delta I know needs water, lots of water. Of course, without that water, a new ecosystem will develop. Perhaps one day others will champion saving that system.

I established my base camp at the narrowest point between Lynx Stand and Lousy Creeks. A strategic location not only because of access to the site from the bottom ends of both creeks but also because most bison migration trails from the delta funneled into the top end of Lousy Creek at what I called Kingfisher Crossing. I watched a young peregrine falcon attempt to kill a kingfisher at this crossing, hence the name. The Kingfisher Crossing area became increasingly more important as my fall headquarters. Springtime travels were centered at a place called Fly Camp Meadows. Fly Camp Meadows was sandwiched between two forks of Lousy Creek. Both Kingfisher Crossing (base camp) and Fly Camp Meadows became, in time, major headquarters for two filming operations.

Accompanying film crews offered renewed opportunities for research, providing me with travel funds and material to study more about wolves and bison. Since government departments had by this time abandoned all field research on wolves and bison, any source of support was welcome. By the fall of 1992 the stage was set for me to assist two filming companies in their work. The first film company to call on me was Tigress Productions of London, England. The producer had contacted me earlier, and together with his cinematographer we set out on a brief reconnaissance trip in the spring of 1992. What the British film producers saw on the first trip impressed them enough to come back for a fall trip, but complications ensued. A Paris-based company wanted to film in the area as well, and they also required my assistance.

While on a field trip in the fall of the previous year, I had met the director, a well-known French television personality. I was canoeing along Lousy Creek when a local guide brought the director into the area for a reconnaissance trip. The French director was fascinated with the possibilities of doing a film. Within half an hour of our meeting, I showed him wolves and bison in the same area. "Magnifique! Carbyn is 'magic,'" explained the excitable Frenchman; "this should be easy." He said he would return next year for more. "Be sure to keep track of the wolves—we need to film them—the world is waiting for the footage," he told me as we parted company. Once back in Edmonton we met again, and I was generously wined and dined by the television executives. They planned to write a major article for the magazine *GEO* and produce a film. My recollection is that I said, "I might be able to help, but who knows about the schedule next spring." After an initial flurry of letters nothing happened, so I assumed this was a dead issue. In the meantime my contacts with the British film crew strengthened, and I made firm commitments to them. After some ten months had passed, suddenly the French project was back on the front burner. I tried to see if I could accommodate both, but the British schedule didn't seem to allow it. I had to decline the French. But "no" was not acceptable. The French team had acquired the necessary funding and was ready to fly across the Atlantic. They said they had counted on my presence; their projects could only be successful if I cooperated. I was in a very difficult situation. I agreed to help out, but only if Tigress Productions was willing. That started a Paris-to-London link, and the end result was that both companies agreed to my involvement as long as working with one did not interfere with my commitment to the other. I thought nothing more of the situation and continued my work at the time organizing an international conference on wolves. Little did I know how my inattention to the Paris/London discussions would influence subsequent events. What started as a "diplomatic exchange" ended up as a clash in programs that I have referred to as the "Battle of Lynx Stand Creek."

At the height of the encounter, this is what I saw— two clusters of people slogging through sedge meadows, both parties heavily laden with expensive cameras. Slowly moving dark forms threaded their way along until the two sets of dots met. I can still see the slow march of the two "battling units" approaching each other, two British photographers across the flat delta landscape being met by a French television crew of five, briefly mingling, then parting. The English, I was told, stared down their French opponents with "polite indifference," while the French threw up their arms in the air and in an emotional Gallic outburst complained about the situation. I was in the background and felt guilty for having precipitated this encounter. How did it all happen and why was I culpable?

I was in the wilderness, far from the stresses of society, yet I found myself embroiled in a conflict between competing business interests. Here I was happily working with the English crew, spending long hours transporting equipment between camps, portaging canoes, looking for bison herds, and finding kills. Much of the time with the English crew was spent in the rain and without encountering any bison herds. Drudgery with little success. I spent far less time with the French, but they enjoyed an incredible streak of good luck. In three days' work the weather for them was always perfect. I spent only one day in the field with the French team, and we saw bison at every turn. They were delighted with the footage they got in a very short time. The highlight for them was filming a bison bull swimming across the creek. Never before has that happened to me in such perfect sequencing. The French crew was there with cameras, sound recorders, and so on, and it all happened in broad daylight. All we needed now were the wolves.

The next day I helped the English, only to be interrupted by a demanding French crew. They wanted more! The French were strung out across the open meadows and heading in our direction. The English film crew was already on their way to set up the blind when they saw the French coming. One of them turned around, waving his arms, shouting—"Quick, Lu, the French are coming, the French are coming. They are coming to get you, as a guide. You are with us. Hide, so that they can't find you! We need to film by ourselves without distractions." I was in no mood to be used as a pawn. I had my own schedule. Little did we know that the French had spotted a herd of grazing bison. The English angrily left to set up the second blind at a bison carcass.

While the English were gone, the French picked their way through the marshes and came to see me. They told me about the bison "just around the corner." I wanted both sides to have the benefit of filming these animals. Had I acceded to the British request to ignore the French, their inexperience surely would have stampeded the bison. I guided the French as close as possible to the animals without disturbing them. Later the English crew could do their filming.

The sequence of events leading up to this particular trip began with my contact with the British on a crisp fall day in the city of Edmonton. It was in the very early morning darkness, at a service station, that I met wildlife photographer Richard Kemp and his assistant, Jonathan Yule. They turned out to be superb companions in the field. Richard, a wiry energetic man, had endured many hardships on filming trips around the world. His latest trip had been to film tigers in Siberia. Before that he had worked in Africa, places such as Sudan, Kenya, and Tanzania, and in Europe. In Spain he produced a remarkable film on European wolves.

They had arrived from England a day before and were eager to get the expedition under way. After quick introductions we picked up their gear at the hotel and set off for the airport to catch our plane to the north country. They dragged with them forty-one pieces of luggage, weighing some 300 kilograms (661 pounds). It was quite a sight. Much to the annoyance of some fellow passengers at the ticket counter of the airport we heaved, item by item, piece by piece, all the gear onto the scales. A commercial plane took us to Fort McMurray; from there we transferred to a Beechcraft for the forty-five-minute flight to Fort Chipewyan.

How different travel to the north was now compared to sixty years ago. Then much of the travel had to wait for waterways to be released from the grip of the winter ice. A train took travelers to Fort McMurray; from there they transferred to scows, large flat-bottomed boats, or later, steam-driven stern-wheelers, and traveled down the Athabasca River to Fort Chipewyan and points farther north. Airplanes make travel independent from all but the most severe weather conditions. Sitting in the comfort of the plane from Edmonton to Fort Chipewyan, I described the scenery below to my traveling companions. Dominating the landscape north of the city of Fort McMurray with its oil sands is the Athabasca River, an important feature of the delta landscape farther north.

Showing my newly acquired British friends the colorful scenes while flying over the boreal forest was a delight. In Fort Chipewyan we were met, as so often in the past, by the warden service of Wood Buffalo National Park. Jeff Dixon, a veteran on the warden staff, came to pick us up. He told us that because of strong easterly winds it was not possible to leave on the four-hour trip by boat to the delta that day. We were disappointed. All three of us were eager to get started. But as a result of the delay we got a chance to fly in a small airplane on a reconnaissance trip over the delta. This was an eventful occasion not only because we saw large herds of bison from the air but also because Jonathan became frightfully airsick.

Jonathan was a shepherd from Norfolk who had spent all his life on the ground and had no experience in small aircraft. Once in the air his jolly face was at first totally absorbed with the variety of wildlife scenes below him as the plane whisked us over the colorful fall landscape of the delta. Ribbons of yellow willows lined the sides of creeks. His broad face was glued to the airplane window. We saw large flocks of migrating tundra swans and snow geese. Then came the bison—small black spots on a golden carpet of sedges. As the plane turned and changed altitude, Jonathan suddenly felt queasy. First concerns were set aside, but as the flight progressed, he became less interested in what he saw below and more preoccupied by the gnawing pain in his head and his grumbling stomach. The next turn was too much—he groped for an airsickness bag and let go. Richard Kemp, sitting beside him in the back seat, helped out in getting the bags and processing them much the same as an assistant in a grocery store. In my role as navigator I glanced back once, then minded my own business. Although not prone to airsickness myself, I knew how infectious the malady can become if you watch others. It is like a yawn—if one person yawns, others follow suit. Richard asked if he could throw the bag out the window and the pilot nodded. With one flick of the wrist out it went. Jonathan heaved again, and I could hear the gagging behind me as all the contents of his stomach were jettisoned into the second bag. As before, Richard reached out to toss the bag from the window of the plane, but this time the bag crumbled in his hand, and a gust of air swept the container back into the plane. Yellowish, green liquid splashed over his face, camera, and the backseat and roof of the aircraft. Moans, groans, and wiping of surfaces carried clearly to the front of the plane. A quick glance backward confirmed my resolve to keep my focus to the front.

"Keep your mind on bison," I prompted myself. Dripping from the ceiling were bits and pieces of Jonathan's partly digested lunch, buffalo burger no less, served an hour before at the Fort Chipewyan Lodge. By the time we returned to the airport, poor Jonathan was white as a sheet; on rubbery legs he staggered to a sitting position on the tarmac. There he stayed in a complete daze for twenty minutes. Another forty minutes of rest in the aircraft's hangar was required before he would even think about moving. Richard and I were invited out for supper at a warden's home that evening. Jonathan could think of nothing but rest. His whole body was shaking and as he told us the next day, "had someone offered to shoot me, I would have told him to go ahead." Poor fellow, but what a good sport. We were able to laugh about it and get on with the next stage of the trip.

The next day was given to preparing for the boat trip to the Lousy Creek area. As always, most of the groceries had been purchased in Edmonton, but some last-minute goods had to be obtained in Fort Chipewyan. What once was called "the Bay" (that is, the Hudson's Bay Store) had been since the late 1980s officially called "the Northern Store," though everyone still referred to it as "the Bay." Over the years a surprising variety of imported food items and dried goods have found there way to the store. This was a far cry from when I first visited the store. In the mid-1960s most goods in the store were staples for the trapper—flour, sugar, lard, and dried goods. Now there was kiwi fruit from New Zealand, grapes from Chile, and tomatoes from Mexico. Like so much in the lives of these northern residents, the south had infiltrated the infrastructure of the northern communities. As Jonathan and I did our last-minute shopping, we walked by the "philosophers' bench" in front of the store and greeted the wise sages passing the time reminiscing about the "old days." The old-timers were not always quite sober. This gathering spot is frequented by the regulars and serves a useful function: it is a social center where the community spirit of the present touches base with the past and sometimes, usually in a derogatory way, contemplates the future. Later that day we met our boatmen, Scott Flett and Jumbo Fraser, loaded our supplies on their trucks, and proceeded to the docks. It took two eighteen-foot Lund boats to transport all our gear, which included two canoes that had to be placed on top of the loads because at the speed these boats traveled towing them behind was impossible.

Lake Claire is a tricky lake to traverse. On foggy days there are places where you cannot see across the lake. Wind can often "seish" the lake level, piling water up in one region at the expense of another. At certain times of the year (particularly in the fall) much of the lake is covered with aquatic vegetation, which makes transportation difficult, as the propellers of motors get tangled in the weeds. A combination of problems marred our trip on this occasion. Shallow water and short choppy waves made travel difficult. As always, a pleasant portion of travel was in the calm waters on Prairie River. Though it was mid-September, ducks still abounded, and bald eagles were frequently spotted gliding along the water's edge.

Still in the area were bitterns, belted kingfisher, and shore-birds. The richness of bird life greatly impressed Jonathan Yule, who was reminded of his home along the Wash in Norfolk, England. I too have marveled at the avian diversity. Except for some studies on waterfowl, almost nothing is known about the bird life in the delta. A study on shorebirds was conducted in the late 1990s, but it was superficial and not followed up. Here, I always thought, would be an opportunity to set up a bird observatory, with a particular emphasis on community involvement. Traditional involvement in resource harvesting by native residents could be redirected to resource monitoring and long-term study. This is a project I have pursued with the local people and with international conservation groups.

Our apprehensions as to how Jonathan would tolerate water travel were groundless. He was not affected by it, which was a great relief for us all. The boat trip took us past the remains of an old commercial fish plant (known locally as John Marten's cabin) and then on to the mouth of Lousy Creek. The shallow waters concerned us, and at one point the whole load of one boat shifted and the wind caught the edge, almost causing it to capsize. We shuddered to think about the consequences. I watched Richard's face. He was probably weighing the consequences of the unthinkable. What if film and expensive cameras and lenses were to get soaked in the murky delta waters? But no disaster occurred and we continued on. Evening set in, so we had to drop our goods off at a location some distance from our planned campsite. As we unloaded, the sun was still shining, but while we were lug-

ging the gear to our campsite, we could see a veil of pre-
cipitation off in the distance—clouds were rolling in from
the west. A small flock of snow geese lifted off the brown
sedge meadows. Their restless behavior indicated an urge
to head south. Seeing the rain coming, we scrambled to
get our tents up and our gear under a tarp before the pelting sheets of water reached us. The summer shower
("clearing shower" as my English companions put it)
lasted for only twenty minutes, long enough to keep us on
our toes and get the camp up in short order. As darkness
set in we could hear the boats of our guides fade into the
background.

Standing on the edge of the willows, I took in a deep
breath of fresh air and thought about how great it was to
be back. I was exhilarated as my eyes sought the horizon
of this flat landscape, looking for its most prominent faunal inhabitants, the bison. Those delightful dark, heavy-
set hulks moving in herds are the center of attention for
both human and wolf. What adventures were to lie ahead
in the next three weeks? To add to my pleasure, I liked my
traveling companions; it would be fun to spend time with
them. Moments like this last a lifetime.

Jonathan was thrilled by the prospect of adding new
images to his collection of paintings. He took a few steps
along a bison trail, rounded a corner, and was met, at very
close quarters, by a huge white wolf. Beginner's luck! He
was excited beyond description. The size, the hypnotic
eyes, and the whiteness of the fur were all impressive. He
wanted to know about weight—I gave him a general
answer. How heavy are the Wood Buffalo National Park

wolves? Not here with me in the field, but many kilometers farther south, in my office gathering dust, I had the answer.

Sebastian Oosenbrug, Warden Duane West, and I kept records on the weights of wolves captured from 1978 to 1981. Upon my return to the laboratory, I sought out the information. It pays to be a pack rat. Eagerly I leafed through yellowing capture sheets that listed males, females, and young of the year in columns. Next I looked into weight records of the wolves transported from Canada to Yellowstone in the U.S. reintroduction program and compared results. The heaviest wolf captured during the 1978–81 study in Wood Buffalo National Park was a 58-kilogram (128-pound) male; the heaviest female weighed 41 kilograms (90 pounds). The average adult male weighed 47 kilograms (103 pounds); the average adult female, 39 kilograms (86 pounds). Pups, captured in midwinter, weighed an average 33 kilograms (72 pounds). Color variation was of interest too. Seen from a distance there are basically three phases—gray, white, and black. Most of the wolves captured in this study were gray, but half as many were also white or black. White wolves were more common in the delta than in other areas farther south of the park, and I attribute that possibly to the proximity to tundra regions. Caribou wolves may have moved south to breed with local wolves. Upon handling wolves, one gets precise information on color—you actually see the great variation up close. Here are some of the descriptions of Wood Buffalo wolves—black, gray black, white, yellow white, blond, brownish gray, gray grizzled, brownish black, gray brown with black streaks. I have never seen a "blue black" in the delta, the very unusual color phase that I noticed in Jasper National Park and again in the Mackenzie Bison Sanctuary and the Hay Camp area within Wood Buffalo National Park. It is a color phase that showed up in the Yellowstone Park wolf transfer as well. In reality a "blue black" is a black wolf when it is still young to middle aged. Black wolves often turn white going through the "blue" stage. I shared this information with my friends that night at camp. I also recalled that in sixteen years in the delta I had only once seen a coyote. Coyotes had been reported as common in the delta during the days of wolf control. My explanation was that once wolves were no longer being persecuted they killed the coyotes. Such occurrences are likely only possible in a relatively simple system such as the Wood Buffalo ecosystem. In more complex systems, one being Riding Mountain National Park in Manitoba and another the Yellowstone system in Wyoming and Idaho, coyote numbers are reduced but not eliminated by wolves. We talked for a long time, past midnight, about many such issues.

The next morning I packed up my fourteen-foot canoe, locally known as a "rat canoe" used for trapping muskrats, and headed upstream while Richard and Jonathan prepared their equipment for filming. Looking after the equipment is a time-consuming business, but Richard was a master of details. However, there was a downside—he was so meticulous it always took him three or four times longer than others to get going. While I was packing, we heard our first wolves howling, a welcoming ceremony—my English friends were impressed. The magic of the howling never fails to impress those who love the wilderness. Before long we saw the wolves. One particularly large male was conspicuous by his black coat and white spot on the chest. He stood at the edge of the meadows, walked a few paces, sat down, and serenely lifted his head skyward. The muted sounds of the howl drifted through the fall air. It was a long, drawn-out howl. Moments later two other wolves responded. The flat delta landscape was a perfect arena for this performance. I was loath to leave, but I needed to check on the migration of bison herd upstream. Saying good-bye to my companions, I struggled to push the heavily laden canoe off the slick delta mud and into deeper water. As my canoe glided through the rushes, I could hear the howling of wolves in the background. I watched the wind playing across the face of the creek, creating ripples that then disappeared into the flatness of the water's surface.

A Chilly Hike

I f Richard was to get the film footage he needed, I had to find bison and wolves. I paddled the canoe to my next destination in search of our quarry. The aspen leaves were turning, and the landscape took on a brilliance that was magical. Everywhere on the creek huge flocks of ducks took off as I approached them in my canoe. Above the aspen trees, skeins of tundra swans winged their way southward in flocks of ten to thirty. The snow geese appeared in much larger and noisier flocks. Unlike the swans, the geese were actually resting and feeding in the delta meadows that day. Only one swan landed on the open water in front of me. My canoe was fully loaded with goods, and there were only two to three centimeters (about an inch) of freeboard left. The craft was well balanced and glided along in perfect harmony with its physical setting. My senses were alert.

I rounded the corner at Lousy Forks and proceeded to the widest and deepest portion of the creek. Here, along a short stretch near a huge beaver lodge, a patch of water lilies brightened the landscape in midsummer. I thought about this plant with its varied cultivars in so many gardens around the world. Even in the wild this plant has a wide distribution, ranging from Africa, Australia, Malaysia, and Europe to North America. Tucked away in a remote corner of the boreal forest, it thrives in buffalo wolf country. All the water lilies have evolved a unique way of producing seed. Each flower lasts only two or three days. During that time it goes through a "sex change," female at first, then male. The male flowers exude a strong odor attracting insects to the two-day-old flowers. These insects, carrying the pollen on their bodies, shift some of their activity to the one-day-old female flowers. Here the pollinators get caught in a sticky substance and thereby fertilize the plant. Many of the insects perish in the process.

There was action all around me. Darting away from the surface of the water was the outline of a northern pike. Remarkable also in the fall are the large concentrations of birds of prey. Bald eagles, merlin falcon, peregrine falcons, red-tailed hawks, goshawks, and smaller accipiters (mostly sharp-shinned hawks) are often seen in the delta. Lousy Creek is one of the best places to see them all in one day. The creek is variable in both width and depth. At regular intervals, regardless of the size of the creek, bison have,

Canoeing my way along Lousy Creek (photo by Jeff Turner)

over the decades, established major crossings, which are conspicuous and not uncommonly wind their way up steep banks. Between our two camps were eleven bison crossings. Canoeing along the river meant that at any bend in the creek it was quite possible to encounter a herd crossing right in front of the craft. It happened often. A marvelous experience.

All bison, including calves, are excellent swimmers, but calves at times are trampled to death at these embankments if herds are pushed across creeks in a state of panic by wolves or helicopters. I once timed a herd of bison crossing the Peace River and calculated that they swam at a speed of about 3 kilometers (1.8 miles) per hour. As I paddled along, I kept looking for fresh bison signs at the crossings and occasionally stopped to check the paths leading from the water's edge to the borderline of the vegetation. One crossing looked promising. It had fresh tracks in the mud, and the water was still turbid and milky—a sign that bison had recently crossed. Sure enough, it did not take me long to find a herd near a trapper's cabin. In my time there was only one cabin along the creek, namely Chief Archie Waquan's place. In days gone by there were several. I have often looked for remnants of old wardens' cabins but never found them.

Two huge bison crossings were near Archie's cabin. The larger of the two had the telltale milky water. A muskrat crossed ahead of me as I directed the bow of the canoe toward the mud bank. I pulled the canoe ashore and walked along the bison trail that crossed the narrow band of willows and aspen. This was a well-known crossing and I was certain the bison would be in the open, as the murky water was still dark and freshly churned up. It is not unusual to see wolves among the herds under such conditions so I cautiously approached the trail ahead. I heard the grunting of cows. Bison ahead! As I rounded a corner in the trail I could see some of the stragglers. A herd of about three hundred animals was heading north. A good indication of things to come. Mission accomplished, I backtracked to the canoe. In a radio message to the camera crew (we had radios by now—a luxury compared to earlier days), I informed them of the presence of this herd. They were to join me quickly as one never knows what kind of wolf-bison actions may occur under such circumstances. Unlike my canoe, theirs had a very small motor. It was powered by a completely noiseless thruster and driven by a large twelve-volt deep-cycle battery. Richard had quite ingeniously set up solar panels to recharge the battery.

Through the magic of modern technology (radios), they could tell me of their whereabouts and activities. Both Richard and Jonathan marveled at the landscape and traversed the distance much quicker than I could. They set up a fly camp near the herd while I continued on.

As I glided through the headwaters of the creek in my canoe, I noticed how much lower the water was this year compared to the year before. In front of me a young black bear walked across a shallow part of the creek, quite oblivious to my presence. Not far from that location I landed my canoe at the water's edge and saw a lynx. Earlier that morning I had heard the howl of a single wolf. Bear, lynx, wolf: three carnivores in one day. What a wonderful sanctuary, I thought to myself, though the northern forests and associated landscapes are not as species rich as the diverse African savannas or the rain forests of southern latitudes. I watched the lynx—it appeared to be a young animal. These medium-size predators fluctuate greatly in numbers within the park. A skilled trapper can kill more than a hundred animals in years of abundance. When fur prices are high, that means a huge income for some. The lynx I watched seemed unafraid of my presence. An interesting study of lynx in the Mackenzie Bison Sanctuary by Kim Poole revealed some remarkable movement records of these northern cats. A ten-month-old male captured on March 26, 1990, ended up being captured in central Alberta by a trapper (southwest of Edmonton) on December 7, 1992. That animal had moved 930 kilometers (577 miles) in a straight-line distance. Likely, of course, its perambulations took it much farther afield. Considering dispersal of other captured lynx in that study, the maximum distance covered was an astounding 1,530 kilometers (950 miles). Who would ever have thought such travels possible? Only through radio tracking were data obtained on that subject. This animal was part of a much larger gene pool, potentially extending all the way from Fort Good Hope in the Northwest Territories to Drayton Valley in Alberta. A U.S. equivalent would be the movement of a lynx from Minnesota to Texas.

Camp had to be set up. I worked quickly as darkness had already set in, but my familiarity with my gear allowed me to get comfortable in short order. Providing shelter is a very basic need. A hole in a snow bank is great during the cold of winter. It provides walls to reflect body heat inward. Tents keep mosquitoes and dew away in summer, not to mention rain. Prehistoric man sought out caves or used animal skins to create artificial cover. North American Indians used buffalo hides. I had the benefit of modern synthetic products. The end result is the same—cover and security. Maybe, I thought, as I looked forward to my security, that is why four-year-olds drape bedsheets over chairs to crawl under during play.

After supper I organized all my gear around me—camera equipment in that corner of the tent, food over here, and clothes at my feet. I then rolled out my sleeping bag and wriggled myself into it. Within minutes the down bag warmed up. At this point I am always overcome by a sense of comfort and happiness. I thought about the lynx and a blissful air of tranquility passed over me as I looked forward to the next few weeks. It was a love affair, and someday I vowed that I would write about it. Who knows what will happen to the wilderness areas in the future? I felt a responsibility to future generations to document how it once was.

Would the wolf packs I had heard last fall in this area be back again? I was hoping that my British friends would get the footage they wanted. What if they did not? Only then did it also cross my mind that the French photographers might be coming as well. They had said they would visit the park in the first week of October but that had not been confirmed, or if it had been, the message never got through to me. Not much concern to me at this point, I thought, as the mission was for my British friends to get their film footage and for me to get information on the fall classified count. These counts identified the composition of the herds, therefore establishing the number of cows, bulls, calves, and yearlings. I also needed to increase my sample size on predator-prey encounters. Who had the upper hand? And under what circumstances? I drifted off into a very deep sleep, only to be awakened at 5:00 A.M. by the magnificent chorus of a ceremonial wolf pack howl. I was drowsy and basked in the soothing sounds.

Over the years I have developed a knack for waking up at a specific time when sleeping out in the bush. But wolves will wake me every time. The howling lasted several minutes and came from across Lynx Stand Creek, less than a kilometer and a half (about one mile) away. It was still dark so there was no point in my trying to see them. I did not know then that the pack was feeding on the carcass of an old bison bull. For the next two hours I drifted in and out of sleep. Getting up in the morning was a bit of a chore as the air was cold and the sleeping bag so very comfortable. In the gray dawn sky I could see the first splash of light creeping up onto the horizon, a promise of days to come, filled with adventures. A single sharp-tailed grouse startled me as it flew through the aspen trees. I once found a grouse dancing ground—but that was long ago. I thought they must have been killed off by the foxes, which are plentiful. For breakfast I made a steaming mug of tea, accompanied by English biscuits and some dry cereal. I was soon joined by Jonathan and Richard; as arranged the previous day by radio, they had walked from their fly camp to mine. We planned our strategy for the day. We decided I should stay while they returned to base camp to get more supplies. The sky was completely overcast, and what was at first a light drizzle turned into a steady downpour. After a reconnaissance of the area I returned to camp and spent much of my time writing in my journal and reading. Toward evening it got colder and the rain let up. A short walk south revealed that the bison herds had left the meadows they were in the day before. I settled back into my tent for the night, listening to sounds the wind made as the tent fly flopped back and forth. As morning came I wondered why the tent roof was bulging and the fly did not flop in the wind any more. I poked my head out and was confronted by a magical winter wonderland. About 3 to 5 centimeters (2 inches or less) of snow had fallen.

I was still not quite awake but got my clothes on anyway. My jacket hung loosely, my shirt was not completely buttoned, and my bootlaces were dangling as I scrambled out of the tent. Suddenly, out of the corner of my eye, I caught a glimpse of a dark streak some one to two meters (three to six feet) above the ground—a peregrine falcon swooping over the snowy landscape and dodging into an area with sedges. Out came a flock of horned larks. The falcon made an unsuccessful strike at a bird. The scene flashed before me in a split second; it was enough to wake me up—the adrenaline pumping through my system. All day long huge flocks of geese and tundra swans passed overhead. Winter was on its way, and the weather that caused snow to fall in my area must have extended northward. I could feel the sinister, foreboding gray of a northern winter coming on. However, there was still a short reprieve before winter settled in. By noon most of the snow had melted. The snowfall had flattened out the sedges and grasses, making it easier to spot wolves, foxes, and other small to medium-size animals.

I stayed at base camp another two days. Being alone in the bush gave me ample time to think. This trip had a particularly sad note as it followed only a few months after my wife of twenty-five years and I had separated. For years we had focused our attention on raising our two daughters. But we were both career oriented, and our backgrounds, temperament, and interests were quite different, so our lives began to drift apart. A flood of memories rushed in as I bent down to tie my laces. My eyes swelled with tears as the sadness set in. A family pulled apart. My perambulations in the bush had contributed to the breakup. My wife's identity with the natural world was closely bound to cottage life in the beautiful Canadian shield country of southern Ontario. One trip together into the delta, I had thought, would capture her imagination as it did mine. But she had not been particularly impressed with this flat landscape, and I could appreciate that when comparing the two areas. One's appreciation of nature is often closely tied to one's youth. Flat, biologically rich areas were part of my growing up in the veldt of Southwest Africa (now Namibia). The spectacular scenery of Jasper's mountains never appealed to me as much as the delta; my wife had been at home in the shield country. The primeval nature of a wilderness landscape unclutters the mind and allows it to focus on basics. The clamor of pots brought me back to reality. A skunk was making its rounds and checking out the camp. Unwashed pots had caught its attention. I have often noticed how tame skunks are in the delta. Not a care in the world it seems.

Richard and Jonathan had extended their stay at the supply camp. I learned later that the wolves we had spotted on our arrival were putting on a performance for them. In midmorning of the second day they saw a large herd of bison approach the wolves' rendezvous site. On two different occasions, I had watched wolves killing calves at this site. As they set up their equipment, they could see the wolves moving toward the herd. They became quite excited about the prospect of filming wolves chasing the herd in an attempt to make a kill, but they were not successful.

On another occasion, as they walked along a line of willow bushes, they spotted something moving through the tall sedges. Four wolves approached a large herd. The two photographers ran for cover. The wolves pushed nine cows and five calves directly toward them. There was an all-out dash for about a thousand paces and then the chase slowed to a canter. Richard and Jonathan had to make a quick decision—should they set up the camera and film the chase, or should they run for better cover so they could remain undetected? They opted to look for cover—it turned out to be a mistake. A single wolf pushed the bison past the photographers but did not persist in the chase. Opportunity missed. Events unfold quickly in nature, and split-second decisions must be made. Whether they will bring success or failure no one can know in advance—and there is no instant replay. All one can do is hope for another encounter, another opportunity, and the good fortune to make the right decision that time.

Richard and I had another chance to film wolves chasing bison at the same location, but again the wolves refused to cooperate. We saw the bison herd in the distance. They were tightly bunched together—always a sign of impending action. We grabbed the camera, tripod, film, and rucksacks on the run and sprinted from camp along a row of willows toward the action. As we got closer, we noticed that the herd had begun to stampede toward us, and we rapidly set up the tripod and filmed as the bison rushed in our direction. We were both out of breath as we sat down to set up the equipment. I kept looking for the wolves, hoping they would be following on the heels of the bison, but they stayed behind. The wolves, for some unknown reason, simply were not interested in continuing the chase. Since the bison herds migrating through this area began to peter out, we decided to move all our attention to the camp at the headwaters of Lousy Creek.

Richard's strategy for obtaining footage was to use blinds. He had successfully produced some twenty wildlife films using this technique. His blinds are homemade canvas riggings, supported by an ingeniously interconnecting yet simple set of lightweight aluminum poles. He would set up his blinds in strategic locations and completely camouflage the canvas structure with grass, twigs, and branches. When we moved from the camp meadows to the new location, we dismantled the set and loaded everything into two canoes. All afternoon the three of us canoed along Lousy Creek. It was a spectacular journey past the splendors of the golden yellow aspen landscape, watching ducks rise in huge flocks and listening to migrating swans and geese overhead. Muskrats swam along beside the emergent vegetation.

On arrival at the second camp, we were met with an omen of great promise. Just after sunset, as the canoe sliced through the mud at the landing site, the deep, loud, hair-raising alarm bark of a wolf sounded a menacing greeting. Great we thought, a promise of events to come. From the nature of the bark I could tell it was a dominant animal. The wolf, it seemed, was in no mood to tolerate our presence in this wilderness setting but had little choice in the matter. I had already set up the tent earlier, so all we had to do was portage our equipment some 250 paces and prepare for supper. That done, we settled in for the night and were soon listening to rain pattering on the roof.

Fall weather conditions change quickly at this latitude. Clouds, in particular, have a habit of rolling in seemingly from nowhere. One is constantly aware of the direction of the wind. A north wind brings cold air and with it migrating flocks of swans and geese. A west wind brings clouds. I listened to wind and rain as I lay in my bed that night and drifted off into a comfortable sleep. In the middle of the night the thunder of hooves was discernible. Was I dreaming or was this real? I whacked my elbow as I reached for my watch. I was not dreaming. The herd was coming closer, a roll of thundering hooves, like the steady staccato of a drumroll. I have often heard this sound in the middle of the night, usually between midnight and four o'clock, hooves pounding on the delta soil like the din of approaching thunder. It gives one an uneasy feeling. The earth shook, accompanied by the steady grunting of the cows. There could be only one reason why they were running like this—wolves. I poked my head out of the tent, but there was nothing except the darkness and gusts of rain pelting my face. The next morning confirmed what we already suspected—about thirty bison had galloped past the camp and in the freshly churned mud were the large prints of wolf tracks. How far did the bison run? Do wolves have an advantage over bison in darkness? Did the wolves make their kill? Possibly, but if so it was some distance away because a thorough scanning of the meadows did not reveal any telltale signs of wolves, ravens, or other scavengers.

The days went by with no wolf attacks or kills. Richard became restless. His company had spent large sums of money acquiring equipment, such as solar panels, batteries, and film, and sending the team over from England. But nature has a way of delivering on its own terms. Wolf chases had taken place twice during our stay, but the cameras were not in place at the time. Now the chases were happening at night. For my own studies, I was very pleased. Information gathered each day added to my experiences and insights, but Richard's peace of mind depended on pleasing his sponsors. He needed footage, good footage. We set out to establish a blind near one of the major bison crossings.

It was raining. Dark sheets of water poured from the sky and all around us was the blackness of a wet, dreary day. The weather matched the darkness of our spirits. Two weeks of effort and no significant results. With heavy, rain-soaked packs we tramped through the mud across Lousy Creek. Deeply imbedded in the mud were wolf tracks, and the howling at night told us we were at the right location. If only we could get the wolves, the bison, and Richard's cameras together.

Richard and I differed on the best strategy for accomplishing that goal. Blinds, Richard told us, were the solution. I preferred to be more mobile. We arrived at Triangular Meadows, an area that fifteen years ago was a huge lake. Richard found a good spot to set up the blind. It was at the same location where, the year before, I had observed wolves at a rendezvous site. Two days earlier I had confirmed the presence of pups and adults at almost precisely the same location as last year. Richard was fussy— the blind had to be at a very precise location, with a view, yet in cover, inconspicuous, yet at a location where animals walked by. "Put some more twigs over there." Twigs were brought and put in place. "Not so many, I've got to be able to swing my lens around to that angle." Then Jonathan spotted a black wolf—"there's one!"—and we looked up.

What a thrill! He was a pup about six months old and already three-quarters grown. The sight of the pup buoyed our spirits. Gone was the tension. A feeling of camaraderie returned. This obviously was a good location for the blind, and we were motivated to get it up quickly.

Jonathan and I left Richard behind while we went in search of other photo opportunities. For the next three days and nights he was a prisoner in very close quarters. The space he crammed himself into was little larger than 1 meter (3.2 feet) square. He had a small stool to sit on and a short-wave radio. BBC news kept him in touch with the outside world. This time the wolves cooperated. In the next few days he saw and heard the pack many times. At one point the largest wolf he had seen approached the blind to investigate. Curious about this strange apparition in its domain, the large white animal moved right up to the lens. Cameras purring, Richard got some superb footage. On another occasion the whole pack assembled in the very early hours of the morning. Richard, still drowsy from sleep, grabbed his camera. The pack members were milling about all around him but the lens fogged up. In the meantime I looked for other opportunities and one soon materialized.

The weather became our ally. What started out as a drizzle changed to snow. This time the snow stayed for two days and then melted away, which was fortunate for us. We were into the first week of October, when freeze-up can make transportation by boat impossible. Jonathan manned the base camp while I was going out on sorties to find new situations for filming and for getting classified counts of bison herds. One evening when I got back from a hike,

Jonathan excitedly reported that he had a skunk in his tent. "A skunk?" I said. "In your tent?" "Yes, and I had no idea how to get the blighter out, so I grabbed short sticks, opened the tent door at one end, and crawled in—the fellow did not want to go so I threw sticks at it." "Throwing sticks at a skunk in a tent is hardly wise," I explained to him. "I know," he replied, "but how else could I get the blighter out?" Fortunately, he had dealt with a young skunk. Over the next two days this skunk and a much larger one visited us again. I showed Jonathan how to live with skunks without getting into trouble. No quick movements, be gentle, and always speak to the animal quietly and reassuringly. Meanwhile we kept in daily radio contact with Richard in his blind. He was getting results, but I kept looking for better opportunities.

I was on a routine canoe outing checking out areas along Lynx Stand Creek. I had not been here before so everything was exciting and new. Because of the two film crews in the area, the wardens at Fort Chipewyan had asked that I stay in touch as they straightened out administrative matters regarding the arrival of the French team. I was to contact the park headquarters at noon this day. At eleven o'clock I landed the canoe and began to hike along a migration trail. As I walked up the bank of the creek and onto a bison trail, I could see myriad wolf tracks in the fresh mud. I followed them. Only half an hour before the scheduled contact with the park, I came upon a raucous setting. Ravens and magpies were teeming in a clump of willows. Sitting in an aspen tree were two large bald eagles. Obviously, these animals were feeding on a carcass. I realized that a pack would be nearby. Yet I had to keep my appointment. I did not want to leave, but I had no choice. Continuing toward the rendezvous site, I came to a creek. The water was knee-high, and to keep my footgear dry I removed my boots and socks and left them on the creek bank. I would pick them up on my way back. I had to cross a wide belt of thistles, but my bare, numbed feet barely felt their sting. My excitement level was so high I believe I could have walked painlessly on a bed of nails. Some fifty paces in front of me, a black mound protruded from a clump of willows—could that be the carcass?

The heavy putrid smell of rotting flesh permeated the air. Inching forward I crouched behind a willow bush. A white body strained against the black carcass. Yes, wolves were feeding on carrion. Could it be a pack? I moved forward to get a closer look. No—there were only two animals. The second wolf was some twenty paces away resting in the tall grasses. Eleven magpies noisily swept down from the trees. They were preoccupied with something around the head of the carcass. Upon closer examination I saw a massive, lavalike flow of fly maggots oozing down the side of the carcass's neck. What a revolting sight! That is what the magpies were feeding on. Slowly, I retreated without disturbing the site and kept my appointment with the park officials. Back at camp I reported the news to Jonathan and Richard, who by this time had returned from the first blind. That evening we decided to move the blinds to a new location.

Richard was a voracious eater. He had an exceptionally high metabolism and could pack away copious amounts of food without gaining weight, which was fortunate. He had little else to occupy his time while sitting for days in his blind. For hours on end he would wait for action to come his way; occasionally he was rewarded for his patience. On the second day a single large white wolf paid a visit to the smelly carcass. This wolf put on an incredible display of strength, lifting the heavy, stiff head of the bison and twisting it around so it could feed on the uneaten lower portion. Richard set up his tape recorder. The wolf grabbed, tugged, and bit into the meat, pulling pieces off the stiff carcass. The bone-crushing teeth ripped into the putrid body of the old bull. The tape recording magnified the gruesome qualities when we listened to the sounds afterward. The wolf left the carcass; then some twenty paces away it flopped down with a thump. It turned around to get comfortable. Finally, having apparently achieved the right position, the wolf rested its head on its outstretched forelegs. After some time the pack howled in the distance. His ears perked up. The wolf stood up, scratched and shook himself. After two hours the pack moved in and the single wolf had to leave. All night long the pack stayed at the carcass, feeding on what was left of the meat. The carcass was being pushed, pulled, and torn apart. The snapping of ribs could be heard as the body was being dismembered. The drawing together of the massive cheek teeth by the powerful jaw muscles resulted in the crunching and cracking of bones. Wolves regularly left the carcass to drink water from the creek. The slip, slop, slip, slop of their tongues slopping up water was incredibly loud. Then suddenly—silence. The pack had left. About half an hour later, new sounds—thundering of hooves. The pack was chasing a herd. Again, drama in the delta. As the noise came closer, there were sounds of grunting and snorting— the ever-familiar call of cows for their calves. It was a calm, beautiful, moonlit night, stars twinkling in their brilliance. But the bison were panic-stricken and running for their lives. We could not tell if the pack made a kill as a result of that chase, but it is quite likely they did.

This episode seemed to confirm what I had suspected all along, that the wolves in the Lousy Creek area will chase and kill calves in preference to other food sources. The pack did feed on the huge mass of meat on the bison bull, but when an opportunity to kill calves presented itself, they appeared to turn to that food source, leaving the carrion behind. On the next day Richard, tired but jubilant, returned to camp. Although he did not get film footage of the chase, he did get some good close-up shots of the wolf feeding at the carcass.

In the afternoon I received word from the park wardens that the French film crew was on its way and wanted to see me. After lengthy discussions with Richard and Jonathan, I decided to spend the next evening with the French crew. But as I soon found out, the French expected my full participation for several days. The following day we were preoccupied with the filming of landscape scenery; I did not get away from the English crew until nearly dark. To get from Lousy Creek (our base camp—the English "fortification") to Lynx Stand Creek (the French "fortification"), I had to traverse a marshy area along a bison trail. Before the drying of the delta, that walk would have been impossible as the whole area was under water. Unless the water regime changes, it most likely will be easy to walk between these two creeks. In fact, by the year 2000 it was a simple task.

I managed to cross in rubber boots without getting my feet wet. When I reached Lynx Stand Creek, I saw that my canoe was missing. The French had borrowed the canoe. I was angry. I had the choice of returning to Lousy Creek before darkness set in or walking to the willow clump where the French were camped. "Well," I thought, "let's get this 'working for the French thing' over with." So I walked on. Not long afterward I could hear the excited chatter of people around a campfire. I called out and within minutes saw a cadre of cameramen, assistant cameramen, sound men, and the director walking toward me—all pursuing their "quarry," namely "the Wolf Man." Our meeting was jovial. The director greeted me with outstretched hand and a friendly slap on the back. "Welcome to camp." Every gesture, every word, every step along the way was recorded on film. I felt a mixture of annoyance and flattery. We walked over to the campfire and the guide brought up a box for me to sit on.

There was a chill in the air and fall-colored leaves were still on the willows. In the background was the bright outline of a quarter-moon, past which two short-eared owls flapped by. In keeping with French hospitality, red wine was served. The director wanted an informal exchange between me and the guide, every word duly recorded on film. The atmosphere was spellbinding. Next to me was a box where instant replay showed the scene as the film recorded it. I looked over my shoulder and was fascinated by the replay in the video screen. "Wow!" I said. "What a splendid setting." My comments were not called for—they quickly removed the box. I was an actor; my words in the interview were being recorded and obviously the stage was set for filming.

After the interview it was time for me to return to the English camp. Easier said than done, as by now darkness had set in. Confidently, I set off on the 2-kilometer (1.2-mile) hike back. The French did lend me a flashlight and ferried me part way by boat, partial compensation, I thought to myself, for having pirated my canoe. Then I set out across country, looking for signs of the bison trail but not finding it in the blackness of the night. This cross-country trek could have been fatal. Instead of the dry trail, I ended up at the edge of a shallow lake. The water temperatures were low and combined with the coldness of air quickly sucked the warmth from a human's body.

I had no choice but to follow my instincts once I had committed myself. I headed into the darkness following a mental compass line across the emptiness of space without beginning or end. At first I had little trouble in making my way across the marsh. Then, slowly, the water got deeper, up to the rim of my boots, then up to my knees. I struggled forward as the vegetation got thicker and the water deeper. The farther I went, the deeper the water. My friends at camp had put out a lantern—a most welcome beacon. I gritted my chattering teeth and focused on the beacon—only about a thousand paces left. In the glow of the flashlight I could make out marsh plants that twined themselves around my boots and caused me to stumble. Closer came the beacon from camp. The water had now reached my waist, but I was determined to keep going, not to backtrack. The water could get much deeper on the next try; I had no way of knowing where the deep and shallow spots were. By now I could hear the encouraging words of my friends. Their voices pulled me forward. "Keep the fires burning in the cook tent," I shouted. I must be getting closer, even though the light seemed about as far away as ever. Then I noticed that the vegetation had changed—a good sign. Sedges, instead of bulrushes, that meant I must have crossed the deepest spot and was now on the other side of this marshy lake. My feet, legs, and body were numb as I staggered on through shallower water. The lantern was bigger and shone much brighter. I staggered onto dry land. Another fifteen minutes along a bison trail and I was at camp. Warm tea, appreciative smiles all around—I was back at my camp with friends. I had made it!

The magic of the evening with the French and the ordeal afterward had given me a lighthearted, almost reckless, feeling. Richard and Jonathan thought I was drunk. The French red wine might have accounted for some of that but I felt completely sober. This led to further complications. When it finally came to the showdown in the field between the French and the English, the war of words between the two factions included reprimands from both sides—and "not only that," said Jonathan, "but you got our guide drunk." "How did I ever get myself into this?" I thought afterward. Here in this pristine setting, caught in a battle between artists from two worlds—the exacting, hard-working, tenacious British and the spontaneous, jovial, free-spirited French. In different ways I helped them both get glimpses into the lives of wolves and bison in the delta. And unlike other "battles," this was one in which both parties won. The competition resulted in their capturing vignettes about Wood Buffalo National Park that the English-speaking world and the French-speaking world would view on film. Millions of people would benefit, and for me it ended with a sense of satisfaction, despite one big disappointment: the French film used footage of Spanish wolves in a Spanish landscape to fill in for Wood Buffalo wolves. Nevertheless I felt we all had accomplished something important and obtained insights into the biological world so rarely explored before.

I left by boat a few days ahead of the English field crew. The French had left much earlier. Because of the exceptionally low water levels in Lousy Creek, we were concerned about how to get the English crew's equipment out. Richard Kemp, a pilot himself, opted for an aircraft. I always disliked the intrusion of aircraft in the area, but necessity called for some drastic measures. I left to attend a conference and felt rather guilty leaving my friends to their own devices. Months later I talked to the pilot who flew in to rescue the expedition. David Smith, or Smitty as he was affectionately known to the locals, was a veteran pilot and did a superb job bringing in the Beaver float plane and taking the expedition back to civilization. He described the exodus to me. The plane landed on a straightway on a wide portion of Lousy Creek. Richard took much longer than planned to get all his equipment packed up exactly the way he wanted.

They surveyed the mountain of equipment before them and debated the best course of action. But there were no choices; they had to catch a plane out—back to civilization. "It will probably take two trips," said Smitty in a reflective tone of voice, "but let's see what we can do." The three of them proceeded to pack the plane, item by item; there seemed no end to packages large and small. That done, they had only room enough left for one passenger. What to do? They looked at each other again. "Well," said Smitty, "Jonathan you go in first and we'll just pack Richard in over on top of you." Impossible, thought Jonathan. Richard's head and torso went in all right and his arms and legs were draped around whatever space could be created by pressing boxes and bags together. Confidently Smitty climbed in. "Well here goes." Fortunately there was a long stretch of straight water along Lousy Creek at that point. The Beaver revved up its horsepower and the veteran pilot guided his machine along the straightway—slowly, ever so slowly the machine lifted out of the water. "I could have aborted liftoff any time before hitting the trees," Smitty confessed to me. It was not necessary. The evacuation of the British forces went off without a hitch.

Not long after my adventures with Tigress Productions, Jeff Turner called me. He was about to sign a contract with BBC-Nature, one of the world's premier nature film productions, for a two-year project to film the interaction of wolves and bison in the delta area. He invited me to participate and I accepted.

A Film in

the Wilderness

One evening in April 1994 the telephone rang. It was Jeff Turner's familiar voice at the other end, telling me that he had secured the contract with the BBC and was "planning our next trip." It was the first of a series of calls in rapid succession—"I will be driving my Bronco, with trailer, from Princeton to Edmonton." "Our assistant will be a young chap from South Africa. Expect me on Sunday night." "Delays I'm afraid, expect me Tuesday." Finally, "we are in Jasper and will be seeing you shortly."

Because of my past experiences, planning for a trip to Wood Buffalo was no longer as chaotic as it had once been. I had all my equipment stored in such a way that I could be on the move with little notice. This time I had an added advantage: Jeff purchased all the required groceries, fuel, and odds and ends. Jeff's young assistant, Anton Pauw, was a twenty-four-year-old South African university student. They arrived in midafternoon on April 27. Jeff came to my laboratory in Edmonton as I was finishing a few reports. The added pressure was useful in helping me keep focused on finishing the task. I was looking forward to abandoning the desk and embracing the tent.

Although we had talked extensively about plans, we needed to finalize a strategy. Jeff and I worked out the details. We planned for a base camp at Lousy Creek, which would provide access into prime bison ranges either by foot or canoe. Then we would set up a fly camp at my old campsite at the forks of Lousy Creek, a distance of about 11 kilometers (6.8 miles) or, measured another way, a two-and-a-half-hour canoe trip. We also planned to use Sweetgrass Cabin, which was about a three-hour hike from the Lousy Creek Base Camp.

In the rush to get to Wood Buffalo and start the filming, I pretty much overlooked the evolution that had taken place in my own life. My studies on wolves now depended on the good fortunes of a documentary filmmaker from across the Atlantic. It wasn't just me. Science funding was shifting throughout North America, and it was pretty much "survival of the creative fund finders." Official responsibilities were now less about science and more about hands-on management. The buzzword at the time was "mission-oriented work." In any case, I had found ways to continue studying in Wood Buffalo even if I was, strictly speaking, doing it in an off-duty capacity.

Some wondered if the film would result in a conflict of interest. Political issues were beginning to take hold, particularly around the question of whether the Wood Buffalo herd should be destroyed due to the diseases that affect them and that could potentially affect cattle. There was also the question of whether I, as a civil servant, was benefiting unfairly—was I on the take? Just thinking about these innuendoes makes me, to this day, furious. I was delighted to have my travel costs defrayed by film companies while they tell the world the story of one of the planet's most remote places. At the same time, I was able to continue small portions of my research and publish scientific papers on my findings. The contributions were minuscule compared to what I had hoped they could be. Needless to say, it was a less-comprehensive research effort than it would have been as an official project. I did understand why the Canadian Wildlife Service wanted to address other problems. The agency was spread thinly over a large area and had many issues to deal with. But it was harder to understand why the park authorities could not see the merits of long-term studies.

The health of the bison herd was again becoming a major political issue, and nothing raises suspicions more than contentious issues. Diseases in the herd were potential problems for cattle, and the rights of native peoples were always of concern to the government. Native rights was an issue I thought we could deal with readily for the filming project. I sought approval from the native community of Fort Chipewyan and assured them that none of my involvement would infringe on their jurisdiction. Jeff and I made a special trip, months in advance of filming, to Fort Chipewyan for clearance. At a meeting with the Fort Chipewyan Wildlife Advisory Board, we were given the green light. One board member noted, "Heck, Lu is one of our elders—no problem." I was honored. So the stage was set for Jeff Turner's filming.

What I call our "BBC Adventure" began in Edmonton. We loaded the Bronco and headed north. After a five-hour trip we arrived in Fort McMurray, a historical jumping off spot to the North. For years goods and passengers were freighted by train to Waterways, Alberta—a town close to Fort McMurray. From there everything was put on barges and transported along the Athabasca River to Rivière des Rochers then to the Slave River (an extension of the Peace River). Rapids near Fort Smith made it necessary to portage goods from Fitzgerald to Fort Smith. After that the barges could travel all the way to the Arctic Ocean via Great Slave Lake and the mighty Mackenzie River. Much of the north was opened up when bush pilots courageously pushed back frontiers. The Canadian bush has been referred to as a hostile environment beyond the clearings around settlements, so the idea of a bush pilot had a connotation of adventure and romance. By the end of the First World War much of southern Canada had linkages forged by a ribbon of railway tracks that permitted goods and people to be transported from east to west. Northern Canada remained remote and inaccessible, yet bodies of water provided opportunities for landing on pontoons in summer and on skis in winter. Flying in northern Canada began in earnest in the 1920s, and a remarkable flight in those days was piloted by Leigh Britnell. In 1929 Britnell set out from Winnipeg, Manitoba, traveled to Great Bear Lake, Aklavik (near the arctic coast), the Richardson Mountains, Whitehorse (Yukon), and Prince George (northern British Columbia), then back to Winnipeg, covering some 15,000 kilometers (9,320 miles). Sometimes I need to recall such events to put my own adventures in perspective. Now daily flights north bring in vegetables from California and fruit from Florida.

Our journey by truck took us through long stretches of boreal forest on roads that run straight for miles. Anton constantly asked questions about the vegetation and other features of the northern Canadian landscape, and I quickly found that I liked his curious nature. These days Fort McMurray is a modern town of thirty-six thousand people—a population that has grown considerably within the past twenty years because jobs were to be had extracting bitumen from the local tar-sands. The three of us found accommodations in a hotel where Anton was appalled by photos of black bears shot and draped as trophies over all-terrain vehicles. The hotel was a favorite stopover for out-of-country guests coming to the Canadian North to hunt black bears. Anton was disgusted with this display of frontier chauvinism—brute force over natures' creatures. Locals, of course, see things differently—nothing indicates that the bear population is declining, and trophy hunts provide income for northern residents, both native and nonnative.

The next day we proceeded to the airport. Anton remarked that he missed black faces. "All white people—seems so unreal." At the airport we were greeted by a friendly young pilot who was originally from Jamaica but grew up in Toronto. I had flown with Mike before, but I was struck by Anton's pleasure at finally seeing a black face. We loaded our gear into the Islander, a small twin-engine cargo plane. The plan was to fly the goods from Fort McMurray to Fort Chipewyan. The next stage was to ferry our freight by helicopter to two campsites, one at Sweetgrass Cabins and the second near Lousy Creek. The latter was to become our base camp. At the same time a large metal box with enough supplies for the fly camp was airlifted to the forks of Lousy Creek. Only the middle channel of Lousy Creek was navigable and even it showed signs of being filled in by vegetation and sediments at certain points. The southern channel is the widest and deepest. At the mouth this channel had been cut off. The land bridge was several hundred paces long, and one could see it rapidly growing wider and more permanent. At times of flooding, though, water still flows across the land bridge and connects Lake Claire with Lousy Creek. As I flew along these channels on supply flights in the helicopter, all the delta lay below me and its history flashed through my mind. How did explorers like Alexander Mackenzie perceive this area when they traveled by canoe in the late eighteenth and early nineteenth centuries? Mackenzie's journal tells us that he "steered west for one of the branches that communicates with the Peace River, called the Pine River." Pine River is now called Claire River and had not been connected with the Peace River for some time (a situation that was changed in subsequent years by having a dragline dig a trench connecting the two bodies of water). I watched it below me, imagining Mackenzie plodding along into the unknown, and realized how risky such adventures were.

On the second trip the helicopter dropped off another load of supplies. In addition to ferrying in supplies, Jeff took advantage of the opportunity to use the helicopter for filming a spring ice jam. We had been told about the jam earlier at the airport by an observer team of Parks Canada staff. Ice jams begin when the ice frozen at the surface of the river begins to crack up as spring approaches. The large chunks of ice crash into each other and eventually, somewhere along a river, they pile up and form a plug. This year the plug had formed on the Peace River along Saw Mill Island, backing the ice as far back as Carlson Landing. The ice jams are key to the health and viability of a large portion of the delta. This major watery system is so fundamentally tied to the total system that an appreciation of how it functions is needed. Floods are partly governed by ice jams.

The mechanics are simple; ice jams act like plugs in a bathtub. Normally water flows easterly down the Peace River then northerly via the Slave and Mackenzie Rivers to the Arctic Ocean. Ice jams may form during spring breakup when great volumes of ice collect along critical junctions along the Peace River. When an ice jam results along the Peace River, water will back up into the delta. Water from the Athabasca River normally flows into Lake Athabasca. Water then flows out of the system via several channels, namely the Chenal des Quatre Fourches, Revillon Coupé, and Rivière des Rochers, and once through other delta tributaries, namely, Sweetgrass and Baril Creeks and the Claire River. Siltation has closed off some of these delta

Aerial view of tributaries flowing from Lake Athabasca into the
Peace River during late April as the ice melts

water bodies at both the source and the mouth. For the
Claire River, siltation at the mouth occurred during the
1950s and 1960s as the result of a sawmill that plugged up
the system. In 1996 the mouth of the Claire River was
reopened by the government. Spring flooding occurs when
the Peace River water level backs into the delta. In such a
case the water flow is reversed. In the past, Mamawi and
Claire Lakes were extensions of a large Athabasca basin. All
the creeks named were part of the delta of the Peace and
Athabasca Rivers. As water levels fell, outlets from the
Peace River to the creeks closed up. Claire and Mamawi
Lakes became separated from Lake Athabasca but are still
connected by water channels. Given an ice jam and enough
water, the Peace River spills over its banks into the creeks
again. The Peace River then feeds the delta and rejuvenates
the region. There is another source of flood waters,

namely the Athabasca River, which during spring floods can push water into the delta from the south.

The Quatre Fourches, Coupé, and Rocher normally carry water out of Lake Athabasca. These rivers can reverse the flow and contribute to flooding conditions when the Peace River is higher than the lake during a flooding cycle. As the Peace drops, currents reverse in the major rivers. When the water from the Peace River reverses its flow, it acts like a dam that holds back the water flowing north and thus causes even greater flooding. Before the construction of Bennett Dam, which was completed in 1968 on the upper reaches of the Peace River, roughly two to four times a decade, huge ice dams would clog the system by jamming certain areas on the Peace River, resulting in massive backflow into the delta. At times walls of water up to several meters high would flow down the creeks and into the delta, flooding the system with heavy silt-laden waters. The silt would settle down and renew nutrients in the soil, raise water levels in small lakes, and flush chemicals from the soil. For bison, all this flooding and siltation meant the sedge meadows would be replenished. Sedges, however, will die if water is retained too long. Here "opening the plug" comes into play. Spring ice melts or is pushed out and the plug creating the ice dam disappears. When that happens, instead of water flowing into the delta, it flows out via the river systems.

The aforementioned process still occurs but not in the frequency nor on the scale seen in past decades. Recent studies indicate that the mechanics of long-term drought cycles may be implicated in changes in the water cycle that have long been blamed on the Bennett dam, although the dam is certainly part of the cause. In any case, from 1968 to 1995 only one major flood occurred and that was in 1974. The impact of the 1974 flood on bison was dramatic. About three thousand animals drowned that year. People who witnessed the 1974 flood spoke of a wall of water rushing up creeks. It caught bison herds completely by surprise and they could find no protection. Some bison were seen stranded on ice floes; hundreds more were seen drifting in the water. Eventually, windrows of carcasses were caught in willow bushes that stuck out of the water surface. Bones littered these areas for years to come. The next flood occurred twenty-two years later.

In April 1994 Jeff Turner and I watched the buildup of ice. He wanted to be sure to get footage for his film so the world could experience the event. Our helicopter set down at Carlson Landing. From the banks of the river we could see the impact the ice jam had on the park. The hydrology—how the water moves and where it is—was dramatically altered. We marveled at the power of the ice jamming up onto a ridge, forcing chunks of ice blocks almost 2 meters (6.5 feet) thick over the riverbanks. It scoured the banks and levees, flattening nearby vegetation. Ice scars were sometimes visible on large trees. We were all hoping this would be the jam that would flood the delta as it did in 1974. We reboarded the helicopter and circled over the jam, which extended some 5 kilometers (3 miles) upriver. We saw silty chocolate-colored water breaching the banks of the Peace River and winding its way through trees into the delta. "Maybe in a day or two we will have to be evacuated," the pilot said aloud. "Let's hope so—this region needs a flood," I replied.

Back at the airport we shared our recent observation with a group of government officials and some others. "Mister, you guys better build platforms and put your stuff up high," observed my trapper friend Reggie McKay, welcoming us at the airstrip. Another bit of news—the warden informed us that "the biologist" in charge of the Mackenzie Bison Sanctuary declared this winter's bison survey invalid because they found only 1,400 animals. The warden had a cocky gleeful smile on his face. There is an ongoing rivalry between the park (National Parks Branch) and the sanctuary (Territorial Government) regarding numbers. Of course part of that rivalry also dealt with the issue of diseased "hybrids" in the park and the so-called pure and disease-free ones in the Mackenzie Bison Sanctuary—offspring of the animals transferred in 1963 along the water system connecting the two nature reserves.

It was time to move to our base camp; we flew out one more helicopter load before setting up our tents as darkness fell. It was April 29 and the sun set around 10:30 in the evening. The days were rapidly getting longer, and the soil was wet with moisture left from the recently melted snow. Small drifts of snow could still be found in shaded areas of the forest. This is a great time of year for foot travel in the delta because the snow is gone but the ground remains hard enough to support the weight of a human. Marshy areas, soon to be almost impenetrable, are firm in April.

From the window of the chopper I saw the precise spot of a special encounter with a bison bull. The old character remains etched in my mind.

I named him Uncle Ben—after an old trapper, long departed but much revered. I was alone at the time. Turning my canoe around the bend of Lousy Creek, I came upon this lonely bull, standing transfixed on the edge of the creek bank. He simply stood and watched. Wolves were howling in the distance, likely hunting bison calves. This tough old fellow would have been easy pickings. I approached the bull; still no movement. He stood like a statue but kept his eyes on me. I came closer. First cautiously, then more deliberately. Not a move. For two hours I kept my eyes on him. Not a step forward or backward did he take. He was fixed to that one spot. I left. The next day he was still standing there. I approached closer this time, and with a self-timer, took pictures of Uncle Ben and me—only feet apart. I was puzzled—what had happened? A veterinarian later told me—likely severe nerve damage from fighting. At camp that night I told Jeff about the incident. He and I had the occasion later to experience another curious episode with an old, lone bull, but that time the outcome was different.

I woke to the sun at 6:15 the next morning. I recorded the details of a "glorious morning" in my journal. I could see the pink sky from my tent through last year's raspberry canes growing at our campsite. I was back in the delta. Soon I heard rustling in the cook tent. Jeff was already up and eager to get going. Hot coffee hit the spot, as did his pancakes. Arrangements were made for the helicopter to bring in the last load of supplies and then to take us back to the ice jam on the Peace River. Not long after breakfast we heard the familiar "chopping" sound and soon saw, dangling some 15 meters (50 feet) below the helicopter, our canoe. It was a curious sight as it swung into place next to the loads already in the meadow.

The day before, I had flown alone with the pilot. He had meticulously briefed me on all the details regarding safety procedures. Once in the air, I asked him how long he had been flying. This was only "the second day on the job since starting at Fort McMurray," he said. Thinking that he had experience elsewhere I asked him if I was his first customer with the new company. He seemed to get busy with something and didn't answer. Later, he turned to me and said, "By the way, why did you ask me about how many people I had flown as paying customers?" "Just routine," I said; "old-timers are survivors—the best to choose as pilots to get the job done." He looked away again for a second, then confessed with a broad, boyish smile, "The fact is you are the second paying passenger—ever." Not the second passenger he had flown on his new job out of Fort McMurray. "What do you mean? Of all your flying time?" "Yes, you are the second passenger I have ever flown." "Well," I said, "it doesn't show."

The helicopter unloaded the canoe and then landed. We met the now twice-as-experienced pilot who immediately told us he was late because he had not been able to get a taxi in Fort Chipewyan to take him to the airport. It was Sunday and the taxi drivers were sleeping in. He ended up walking 7 kilometers (4 miles) to the airport. Taxi drivers aside, people in the Canadian bush do what it takes to live their lives by their own schedules. After apologizing for being late, the pilot started his machine, and Anton, Jeff, and I joined him in the helicopter. We were treated again to a detailed lecture on safety precautions, location of the emergency locator transmitter, safety gear, and so on. "The chap is still doing everything by the books," Jeff whispered into my ear. We were at the ice jam location within six minutes. These copters can fly 200 kilometers (124 miles) per hour. As we circled over the river, we could see that the ice jam had broken up. Only one branch of the river around Saw Mill Island was still plugged with ice; the other side was clear. All the ice that had backed up to Carlson Landing was gone. Nevertheless, Jeff still wanted pictures of ice chunks along the shore and icebergs floating down the river. The helicopter pilot found a small spot to land and cleverly maneuvered the machine into place.

We clambered out of the helicopter, heavily laden with cameras, and began filming. What a difference twenty-four hours made. The water level had dropped 5 meters (13 feet); the swift current carrying huge ice chunks, often laden with logs, roots, and mud. I trustingly clambered onto the ice, which was still welded to the shoreline. Jeff joined me, but he was burdened with his huge camera and tripod, which together weigh 25 kilograms (55 pounds). Anton came down to hold the camera while Jeff sought safe footing to take photos from a different angle. We thought our only worry was the slipperiness of the ice. We hadn't considered that the candled ice we walked on, which had been pressed together by the force of the river, would have crevasses between layers. The current from underneath eroded open areas, leaving gaps that were covered by thin sheets of ice, undetectable to the topside observer and quite dangerous to walk on. The ice floes were huge and appeared to be quite solid. Jeff took a step and we heard a yelp. I turned and saw him quickly disappearing from sight. He went down in seconds, only the top of his hands flashed out of the hole into which he disappeared. My first fear was that the current underneath would sweep him into the river. Fortunately at that point the ice chunks were resting on soil and Jeff's feet struck land. We pulled him out none the worse for the incident, but it could have been disastrous.

As the filming continued, huge chunks drifting by were captured on celluloid for the world to see. The pilot was getting nervous. He had radioed to base saying the operation would take about half an hour, and we had been at it for a good hour and a half. While the helicopter was on the ground, it was impossible for people to track his movements or current location by radio. Flying helicopters in bush country is risky business, and safety regulations require constant checking of the movements of the machines. It was with some relief that our pilot finally saw us getting cameras back into cases and walking toward him. As we lifted off, we had one more good look at the ice jam remnant, the flood of the decade that did not come to pass. It broke too soon. Months later Willie Coutereille, a park employee, told me, "Had the jam lasted one more day, we would have been in business."

Upon returning to camp we wanted to check out sev-

Jeff Turner after falling through the ice on the banks of the
Peace River

eral more areas around Baril Lake for bison herds. In all the
flying in the last two days we had only spotted one small
herd of 15 animals. What had happened to the bison? The
winter's survey by the warden revealed that only 800 animals were seen in the park. Two winters ago there were
1,400 animals—twenty years ago 8,000. These figures were
depressing. I thought about the political implications of
these facts, how they would support the suggestions that
the herd needed to be culled of diseased animals and be
replaced by animals from outside. Still, it seemed to me
that other factors were at play, and disease was getting
more credit than it deserved. Everyone in the official world
(or at least most of them) had a fixation on diseases. I found
it disappointing that few, including prominent biologists,
had so little interest in the ecological system.

After supper I went for a walk along Lynx Stand Creek. Memories of years gone by came to mind as I rounded different bends in the creek. Nowhere in the fresh, recently exposed black delta soil was there any evidence of bison tracks. The herds were likely still on their wintering grounds farther north and east. Everywhere I looked there were large, fresh tracks of wolves, sometimes right next to the tiny imprints of muskrats. Spring is a time of muskrat dispersal. All winter long these rodents have to survive in their ice-locked landscape. Fall houses are built to give them a place to stay. Up to a dozen or so muskrats, I was told by Reggie McKay, will use a single house. As winter progresses the "rats" will find cracks in the ice, which they keep open; then they come to the surface, bringing with them vegetation to eat. The wolf tracks I saw along an old bison trail were a good sign. "They must be back at their den," I thought. I try not to disturb wolves at dens, and consequently I never pinpointed the exact locations of the dens. Still, I had a rough idea. All tracks led to and from one area. Year after year I had seen tracks at this spot in the spring, and I suspected wolves had been raising their pups near here, as long as the area had not been flooded.

Swans and snow geese flew overhead in the evening light as I returned to camp. This must be the toughest time for wolves I thought. Ten thousand geese are of no use in the air, and when they land, they do so with safety in numbers. Most of the bison calves were not born yet, and the herds appeared to have dispersed. Waterfowl were returning, but few, if any, had begun to nest, so an easy meal of eggs was not at hand. The main sources of food for wolves, and for black bears as well, were carcasses of mostly old bulls and some cows that never made it through the winter.

As I crossed the area between Lynx Stand and Lousy Creeks, I scanned the horizon with my binoculars and spotted five bulls. Lumps of winter hair still hung from their coats. I was hoping that soon these meadows would be filled with grazing herds of cows and calves. With May approaching a few calves were being born somewhere, but most were still within the womb as the peak time for calving was still weeks away. It was frustrating not to have a better knowledge of the whereabouts of the herds or of their activities and movements at this time. Looking at the brown sedges and grass, I realized that from the time of conception to the time of birth—which lasts nine months—bison cows are scavengers of a sort, feeding much of the year on dead grasses and sedges. The irony struck me, that of feeding life with spent life. Only during a few months is the grass green in Wood Buffalo, a time when the calves are growing rapidly.

I reached camp that night and shared my observations with my friends over a cup of coffee. Why were the bison herds not back yet? Will it damage our chances for successful filming? All our equipment was still packed in boxes and various other containers, so we could move with relative ease. Would it be better to establish camp elsewhere? Jeff was inclined to move. I was against it. We decided to stay, and it paid off in the long run. We planned the next day's activities and went to bed. As it approached 11:00 P.M., I heard a single wolf howl in the distance. Sometime around midnight we heard an entire pack.

The next morning we set up base camp. Our cook tent, which doubled as the living quarters, was located at my traditional camping site. Every spring and most autumns for nine consecutive years I had come to that location. Now for the second time an international film crew was to use it as a base camp. More luxuries, I realized, around me this time than at any other time. The cook tent was fitted with a wood stove, a metal table, and a two-burner propane stove. Boxes served for storing food and equipment. Park regulations required that we surround it with an electric fence to discourage bears. In addition to the Lousy Creek base camp, we also had retained the camp at Sweetgrass Cabins.

The Lousy Creek Junction area was a major summer range for bison and thus a prime place to search for the herds. Yet they had still not reached the site by mid-May. It was almost time to get discouraged. On a cold, wet, and windy May 16, we paddled two canoes from base camp to set up the fly camp at the Junction, hoping we would soon see the bison arrive. I was of little use to the crew, owing to my recurring back problem. Anton recognized my agony and worked twice as hard to give me some relief. The canoe was laden with heavy equipment, and he strained against a strong wind as he paddled.

We set up two tents just before it rained, and I crawled painfully into my sleeping bag. All night long it rained, and I drifted between melancholy and nostalgia, between thoughts of the good and bad times in my life. I recalled other visits to this site. Foxes denning in that corner of the meadow, wolves killing a calf over there, a large bison herd stampeding along that row of trees—so it went. In the morning I looked out into the dreary landscape; the gray skies matched the rest of the terrain, and I wondered how such a barren-looking place could be so full of life.

Later that morning we returned to base camp and walked along the Kingfisher Crossing, northward to the Sweetgrass Cabins. It was time for me to leave. I had to return to my work in Edmonton. Jeff and Anton were settled in now and their work was before them. The bison came back, as I had predicted they would. On several occasions during the next three weeks, Jeff and Anton filmed wolves attacking herds. Though these were scenes I had witnessed before, how I wished I could be there to savor the fullness of the events. Yet when I watched the drama unfold on film, I knew I was seeing what the world would see. And it was real, even magical, the next best thing to being there.

The Old Bull

Summer passed and autumn approached. The filming project turned out to be a great success. Jeff's planning and execution were well in hand, and the wolves and the bison cooperated. Together we also got the classified counts I needed for my research. Jeff had a picture in his mind as to what other dimensions he wanted for the film. Filmmaking, I learned, is a highly creative process. Needed still were sequences that captured the change of season from late summer to fall.

On September 12 Jeff arrived at the park. My committee work on the swift fox project prevented me from joining him until later. Restlessness set in as I waited for the appointed time. I was eager to head north. I boarded the Greyhound bus, with all my gear, and headed in the opposite direction of the geese on their way south to the wintering grounds. The charter plane to Fort Chipewyan had a regular mix of passengers that commute back and forth from that isolated hamlet. Some dreamed of all-weather roads into that community, but I liked it the way it was. Being isolated gave the village a charm and a character all its own. Scott Flett met me at the airport. We went straight to the docks, loaded the small power boat, and headed off to the delta.

Scott maneuvered us through the rafts of ducks and the few straggling swans still remaining from the fall migrations. There were perhaps fifteen swans left in the various bays of Lake Claire as we motored past. He talked about the great snow goose migrations, saying that this year's had peaked around September 15. With the geese and swans mostly gone, the waters were left chiefly to the ducks. As we entered Lynx Stand Creek, I marveled at how it was covered from bank to bank with large rafts of ducks. Our boat raised them, and they flew off at a low angle over the surface of the water. Not all could fly fast enough to stay ahead of the boat, so they plunged downward, splashing into the water and disappearing into the deep. I feared that Scott might suck some of them into the prop, but he knew what he was doing, and I never heard the prop sputter nor saw a gush of blood and feathers in our wake.

Jeff met us at the landing of the creek with his brother, who had come to help him until I arrived. Jeff's brother boarded Scott's boat for the ride back to civilization, and after waving good-bye we hiked back to camp. I could not believe how bone dry the usually marshy land was. There was solid footing between Lynx Stand and Lousy Creeks. In front of the camp, where once there was a lush meadow with up to 2 feet of water, was a brown mass of vegetation in an arid environment. The delta appeared to be in terrible shape. I expected sedge meadows with the associated mix of aquatic birds. Instead I was staring at parched, mud-cracked soils, devoid of any kind of vegetation. These worsening conditions had not gone unnoticed by the parks administration. The residents from Fort Chipewyan too had expressed concern about the conditions. At the airport I had noticed a massive poster that displayed charts and information about ecosystem management and what great things were being attempted to save the delta. Apparently they were not yet taking hold. The area was more like a desert than a river delta. All the poster pronouncements, "window dressing of officialdom," had no impact on the real world. The huge dam built on the Peace River was thought to be the culprit, and corrective measures had not yet been taken to counteract its effect on the delta.

The first evening we spent time getting caught up on each other's news. I wanted to know everything Jeff had seen and he wanted me to bring him up to date on what was happening in the outside world. That night I lay in my tent listening to the breeze blowing through the willows. Leaves were gently falling on the canvas, creating a pattern that resembled a patchwork of shapes on a silk cloth. Soothing sounds and images, and I soon drifted off.

Even though it was October 8 the weather was still splendid. Jeff reported that the aspens had changed color a few weeks ago and he had filmed them at their peak; we were well into the feeling of autumn. The temperature of the lake was dropping, which meant that freeze-up would soon begin and the lake and creeks would no longer be accessible by canoe. There were times in the past when I would have had to leave the Lousy Creek area before freeze-up. But Jeff had arranged for us to leave by helicopter.

This is a critical time for bison. If they cross bodies of water while the ice is too thin to carry their weight, they will break through the ice and drown. Another problem is simply finding water. What happens if all water is frozen and the snow has not yet fallen? How can the animals get enough moisture to live? On the other hand, freezing temperatures bring solid footing for bison, allowing access to foraging areas otherwise out of reach. Changes in the environment can be a mixed blessing.

On this trip Jeff and I were without Anton's help. Jeff needed a paddling partner, so I needed to count on good behavior from my back. After a day of exploring the ends of Lousy Creek by canoe, we headed off to the meadows near our fly camp. On the way we checked all the meadows on both sides of the creek. To our consternation, there was little sign of bison herds anywhere. Jeff had learned of a new technique. A local trapper had told him to climb willows in order to see the bison herds in the delta. When Jeff broached the subject, I was skeptical and replied with something like "well O.K., if you must, give it a try." We did and I was one-upped by the filmmaker. At Garbage Point Crossing we stopped to check for bison by climbing a tall willow bush with thick branches. (The point got its name because of the trash that has accumulated there from generations of duck hunters using it as a campsite.) We wedged our way upward and got up about three meters (ten feet) above the ground. Even though the delta is very flat, a bison herd of a hundred or more animals can hide in the tall sedges or in small dips in the landscape. Why had I not thought of this technique before? During the studies

Jeff Turner using a willow perch to get a better view of bison herds in the delta

with Tim we were able to see much better from the tower. I wondered why I hadn't made the simple connection earlier. At the extreme end of the delta, close to Lake Claire and near the west end of Sweetgrass Creek meadows, we could see a few black specks at the curvature of the earth. As we strained our eyes many more dots popped into view. A large herd, looking like tiny black spots in a yellowish brown landscape, was grazing along the shores of Lake Claire. The last herd, we thought, that was still on the summer range.

It rained the next morning. I listened to the steady patter on my tent all night, wondering if by morning it would turn to snow. It did not. Everything was miserably wet and I put on my clothes as quickly as possible and went to the cook tent. Jeff, in his pup tent, was still sound asleep. I lit a fire in the cookstove. Within minutes it was toasty warm and I put on the coffee. The delicious aroma wafted over to Jeff's tent and I could hear him stirring. "Great, the coffee is on," he shouted. The rain continued all morning and we debated whether to go out. "A good time to catch up on our notes," Jeff remarked, and I gave him no opposition. I looked out into the meadows cloaked in a mantle of cold, gray mist. Unfriendly, foreboding, it was a miserable day in the bush. I clutched the steaming coffee mug. It gives you solace, warmth, and comfort. Nothing compares with the feeling of contentment and gratefulness provided by a Cree native wall tent with a wood stove and grub on such a miserable day.

The weather changed and by noon the rain had stopped. We set out by canoe to the north toward Triangular Meadows where we estimated the herd would be. On our way we passed an active beaver lodge from which a large food cache extended out into the creek and hampered most of the creek's flow. Farther on we sighted the white heads of three bald eagles sitting in an aspen tree along the creek. They were likely hunting for waterfowl. Even though the time to migrate was past its peak, late ducks were still in the area. When we arrived at a favorite low water point, a good place to cross, we saw that it was now more like an engineered crossing. The water level was so low one could cross in shoes without getting wet feet.

In the shallows of Lousy Creek we spotted six lesser yellow legs, an elegant shorebird aptly named because of its long, bright legs. They were hunting small fish that were forced into the remaining waters. The fish were in serious trouble. Usually yellow legs prey on invertebrates; it's unusual to see them prey on vertebrates. The yellow legs dashed back and forth, pounding their beaks into the frenzied water. The fish were swimming for their lives, but one after another they fell. The yellow legs stabbed the fish with their beaks. Once dispatched, the fish were flipped up into the air and caught in the open mouth like peanuts. A wavelike motion in the throat was the last we saw of each unfortunate fish. We took a few photographs then set out to find bison herds.

I thought about the differences and similarities between yellow legs and wolves. Instead of a single victim when wolves are hunting, when the yellow legs struck the dead numbered in the dozens. And each yellow legs was the sole executioner and the single beneficiary of the morsel acquired. It's also hard to see how the fish might hurt the bird, whereas a bison has the potential to inflict serious harm upon a careless wolf. But the similarities are there; predator and prey, life and death. Jeff and I felt no pity for the fish. How different our emotions when watching the plight of bison pursued by wolves. Our reaction to the yellow legs darting around chasing the confused fish was akin to an audience watching the Keystone Kops chasing a band of petty thieves on a slippery floor.

We moved on, thinking little of the distraction that had briefly amused us and after a long hike reached the next meadow. We saw nothing but blank yellow vegetation as far as the eye could see. Except for the bison he and I had located the day before, Jeff had not seen any bison herds for more than a week. He was anxious to meet up with bison so he could get the film footage he needed. We had traveled about 18 kilometers (11 miles) that day, hiking and canoeing, and so far it had not paid off.

We returned to the canoe, crossed the creek, and checked out the south meadows. I decided I should snap a few photographs of the yellow legs for my growing slide collection. So I returned to the mud flats and Jeff went in the opposite direction. Hardly ten minutes had gone by before Jeff returned quietly along the trail. His movements were different. He approached cautiously and motioned for me to stay still and look toward a bush as he put his finger to his lips. Obviously he had seen something. In a whisper, as he got closer, Jeff told me that he had run right into a pack of wolves on the trail. He described the lead wolf as a "massive, awesome, magnificent beast" all furred out showing no fear whatsoever. He put up his hands with six fingers, then again pointed to the bush beside me. I got the message.

Cautiously I left the mud flats and climbed up onto the bank. There, among the poplar trees, some thirty paces away, I could see the partial outline of a wolf. Jeff approached and whispered, "There are five more; they were all around me." We tiptoed over and picked up the cameras, then carefully walked back to the scene at the end of the trail. On our way out we saw one wolf drifting through the tree stems like a passing shadow. That was the last we saw of the wolves that afternoon. We got a close enough look at the animals to identify them as part of the Lousy Creek Pack. We were close to the center of their range.

We continued out to the meadows and finally saw two bulls. They were about three hundred paces apart. One was resting, the other standing. Jeff recognized one, a crippled bull with a malformed left hip that he had seen two weeks earlier. Its left hind leg appeared to be nonfunctional. Why had wolves not killed this "three-legged" animal? I reminded Jeff of my earlier experience with Uncle Ben and was sure that I could readily approach this one too.

I wanted to see how debilitated this "old bull" really was. Jeff would document the event with his camera. I slowly advanced. The bull stared at me but did not move. I got closer and he raised his tail. I stopped to gauge his reaction. Then I advanced again. Again the tail went up. Previous experience had taught me to read all the danger signs. I advanced within four paces—then stopped. His heavy head swung around and I could read his intention. Just as I was about to leave he lunged at me. In a moment he gained about a pace. My adrenaline shot up, but there was a short delay before my legs moved. I felt like I was paralyzed. Then, almost instantly, I reached top speed. Even at that I felt I should be running faster. The bull continued for a few more steps and then, to my relief, stopped. Jeff never missed a frame. He was ready to capture Carbyn's last stand.

As we made our way back to the canoe, we discussed the experience. In all my years working with bison, this was one of only two episodes in which they had displayed aggressive actions toward me. On countless occasions I had been yards, sometimes only feet, even inches, away from bison. I had approached males and females of varying ages at different times of the day and different times of the year, though never in July and August, which is the mating season, also known as the rut. I felt confident that I could read the signs of danger and avoid conflict. This one was an exception. I will never forget the flash of white in this old bull's eye. He epitomized the toughness of his kind. Old, diseased, crippled but determined. I would hate to be a wolf and have to face this foe to make my next meal. The courageous lunge was proof of the strong drive and evolutionary programming to survive. The species faces great odds in this hostile environment with floods, cold winters, deep snow, fires, biting insects, and marauding wolf packs. Nothing but man, it seems, can dim the future of these herds in the north woods.

The next day began sunny but cold. We set out by canoe for Fly Camp Meadows. The leaves were almost all gone from the aspen but some of the trees still had a veil of yellow. Aspen are cloned, the clumps connected by a common root system, and the "family" groups show their relation to one another. All the vegetation along the creek was brownish or yellowish, giving the landscape a golden appearance. Warm rays of the sun cast a glow over it all. We felt at ease. Everything seemed serene. But that was to change quickly. Toward the west we saw a dark, massive cloudbank rolling toward us. It looked as if a snowstorm was approaching. The wind picked up, pushing gusts of air

Walking up to the "old bull" (photo by Jeff Turner)

into our faces and slowing our efforts to paddle the canoe. The clouds raced across the sky and soon we were engulfed in gray. The sun was obscured and the temperature dropped. I had neglected to pack warm clothes that morning and regretted it now.

We proceeded to check out the meadows on either side of the creek at two very large bison crossings. There was nothing at the first crossing except fresh wolf tracks clearly imprinted in the black delta mud. At the next crossing we left the canoe by the creek, proceeded up the bank, and moved out through a strip of aspen trees to the edge of a very large meadow-marsh complex. Jeff climbed a tree to get a better view. I checked the horizon with field glasses from the ground and could see neither wolves nor bison.

By now we had circled back to the site of a familiar balsam poplar tree with big branches. It had become our favorite lookout for finding bison herds at Crane Creek. Jeff was just getting settled in his aspen perch when I decided to howl. I thought howling might give us a chance to see wolves and verify the presence of a pack in an area where the tall brown vegetation rendered them invisible. Success was immediate. Out in front of me, no more than 150 meters (500 feet) away, eleven white, black, and gray heads popped up out of the grass and the wolves came running straight for me. The tails were up. The howling alarmed them; they probably thought a neighboring pack was invading their territory. Jeff and I saw them in the same instant. I retreated to the canoe to get my camera. It was the Lousy Creek Pack again, but they were just over the border that, we had believed, separated them from the neighboring Fly Camp Pack. The pack, silent and with tails up, seemed ready to challenge the "other pack," clear evidence that my howling was good enough to pass as that of a wolf. With challenging postures, they walked in the direction from which the howl came, namely me. As soon as I returned with camera in hand, the wolves noticed the mistaken identity and retreated. They returned to where they had been lying in the sedge and milled around. Two adults ventured back, but none appeared overly concerned about our presence. Had we been hunters with rifles in hand, I am sure the reaction would have been quite different. From up high Jeff scanned the horizon and could see two bison herds, still far off in the distance.

The pack set off to the northwest leaving two pups behind. The pack was now five larger than the day before, having added three pups and, curiously, two adults, a large white wolf and a black wolf. The white animal we knew as a member of the Fly Camp Pack. This appeared to confirm the theory that some individuals can readily go back and forth between packs and be accepted in both. That raised another question—what would happen if the two neighboring packs clashed? How would the large white wolf respond? Perhaps the two packs were actually only two subpacks in which different females produced litters.

From his perch Jeff saw the pack move along Crane Creek. He came down from the poplar and we got our gear rearranged and followed. After an hour's hike we came to a bend along Crane Creek. Again Jeff climbed a tree, this time a much smaller willow bush and scanned the horizon. There was nothing apparently close by. He asked me to howl. Again the wolves responded by raising their heads out of the long yellowish grass. The pack was resting along Crane Creek next to three large bulls. Obviously the bulls did not perceive the wolves as a threat. Why did the wolves bed down next to the bulls? I can't say, but speculation leads me to a couple of possibilities. Perhaps wolves find comfort being in the presence of their favorite prey. Another possibility is that wolves use bulls as decoys. Invariably when large cow-calf herds see bulls in the distance, either the bulls are attracted to the large herds or the large herds move to where the bulls are. In either case it increases the possibility for the wolves to make contact with the cow-calf herds.

Jeff and I crossed Crane Creek and carefully approached the bulls. The wolves were not yet visible. The bulls were grazing—a difficult position for us to get close to. We waited until they rested. Soon two lay down but the third continued to graze for some time. After half an hour the third bull lay down as well. We moved in. Carrying our heavy loads, we crept forward in a crouched position.

There was very little cover in the open marshes, but the sedges formed a screen. We finally reached a clump of sedges and set up our cameras. We decided to move forward "just a bit more." It was a mistake. As we inched forward, a white head popped out of the grass. Almost instantly eight more heads came up. They saw us and took off as we stood there watching. Jeff did get some footage of one wolf standing next to a bull, both eyeing each other. Ultimately that piece of film became the title sequence for his classic BBC film. These were the same wolves as before, but our behavior was different and they responded accordingly. Creeping up to them meant potential danger. Just walking around upright and nondirectionally was interpreted as being nonthreatening. At least that was my reading of the mind of the wolf.

We returned to our canoe and pushed off. It slid silently on the soft mud into the murky water of Lousy Creek. As we headed north toward base camp, the last rays of the sun shone through the aspen forest lining the banks of the creek. Large rafts of ducks pattered ahead as they took flight. With each flock we invariably saw a sitting bald eagle surveying the scene. As the sun set, a chill filled the air, and a brilliant white half-moon appeared through the veil of bare aspen twigs. Four river otters were playfully tumbling in the water. They were the first otters I had seen in this creek and I never saw them again, leaving me to wonder about where they came from and where they went.

Nature's bounty that evening seemed to have no limits. The pack of wolves we had watched in the meadow near Fly Camp had also returned to the creek. A long mournful howl came from the adult left behind with the pups. A deep-throated howl, hoarse and guttural at times, responded. The second wolf was no more than two hundred paces from our canoe. From just fifty paces away we then heard a more melodic, high, resonating response. Slowly, very slowly, we dipped our paddles in the water. I kept up a regular dialogue with this wolf. Gently I howled. The response to my howl was almost instantaneous. I kept it up for about five minutes.

That evening we were treated to a wide range of wolf vocalizations. The howl we heard was pure toned and at the longest end of the range of wolf vocalizations. It is likely used when a wolf wants to communicate with its kind when separated by two hundred paces or more. Howls, it appears, can signify a happy social occasion. Growls on the other hand are low-pitched, coarse, guttural utterings, given in aggressive situations at close range. A snarl is a particularly intense form of a growl, uttered during abrupt changes in aggressive encounters. A growl, ending in a bark, can send pack members running or pups seeking the shelter of dens. The wolf's bark, different from the barking of dogs, is a brief, coarse, low-pitched utterance given in usually hostile or threatening situations. Hearing it can be a hair-raising experience. Whimpers, on the other hand, are high-pitched, pure-toned forms of communication given in greeting when two wolves are reunited. I once howled at wolves and had three pups return my vocalization and rush toward me, whining as they approached. Sometimes the wolves will gather and engage in a long series of whimpers that turns into a drawn-out whine.

Jeff wanted to get a close look at the wolf along the shore of Lousy Creek, intrigued by its continual response to our howl. The animal was so close I imagined we could hear it breathe. Ever so slowly we landed our canoe. It was getting dark and we strained our eyes to see the wolf in the bush. I continued to howl and get responses, but the canoe made a soft, sliding noise as we hit some mud and instantly the responses stopped. The wolf evaporated into the broad expanse of darkness. We went on our way. For the next fifteen minutes the chorus of single, duo, and pack howling continued all around us. The fall air made the sounds ring with wonderful clarity, and Jeff was sorry he did not have his sound recording equipment on hand. It was late when we got to camp.

That night winter set in. In the morning all the meadows around us were covered with a glistening blanket of hoarfrost. As the sun rose on the horizon at eight o'clock, the rays reflected a myriad of crystals on the long grass and sedge stems. We packed our canoe and set off through a thin sheet of ice on Lousy Creek. For the first 500 meters (1,640 feet) our canoe had to serve as an icebreaker. The sound was grating on our nerves and certainly would announce us to any resident wildlife. Fortunately, as the creek widened out, there was an ice-free channel in the center of the creek. We decided to go all the way to our fly camp, 11 kilometers (6.8 miles) from the base camp. Along the way we again checked on either side of all major bison crossings, in the hope of finding bison herds and wolves. There were eleven significant crossings from the mouth of Lousy Creek to the upper end. Most of the crossings no longer receive the traffic they did when the area contained some five to eight times as many bison.

When crossing, bison churn up the silt-laden water. The silt later settles out at the edge of the crossing and shallow areas form. Emergent vegetation grows on it, eventually forming a dam across the creek. In a short period of time those areas will completely fill in and cut portions of the creek off from its main branch. On our way to Fly Camp Meadows we were again amazed how much the water levels had dropped within a year. The high water marks were clearly visible on the emergent vegetation along the shoreline. The upper end of the main branch of Lousy Creek, now the only access to Lake Claire, was shallower than the canoe paddle blade. At each stroke we struck the soft mud underneath. Some see this filling up of creeks and waterways as a blessing. "Just think how many motorboats there would be everywhere if the water was deeper," a friend once remarked. He had a point, but I longed for the "good old days" when Lousy Creek was a creek and not a channel choked with aquatic vegetation.

As we paddled back to camp, we came to the sad conclusion that the ice was signaling an end to our trip to the delta for that season. Soon the rivers and lakes would be frozen. I thought about how, when trapping was a common way of life, the changes in the seasons directly affected the native community in Fort Chipewyan. For the trappers, fall was a time of activity. Nets had to be retrieved, untangled, and repaired so that enough fish could be caught to feed the dogs that patrolled the traplines. Food and equipment had to be transported to the trappers' cabins. Wood had to be chopped; dirt that was brought into cabins by mice had to be removed; dogs had to be readied and leaky roofs repaired. Then with freeze-up, winter trapping began. Trappers knew their area intimately. There were beaver ponds, conifer stands, and special habitats that would yield specific species of furbearers. Some of the men would return to Fort Chipewyan by late December, staying there until March and avoiding the bitterly cold months of January and February. Days are short in winter this far north, and snow can be quite deep; fur-bearing animals tend to move less in the depths of winter. The combination of severe cold and lower capture rates were incentives to stay in the village. But some stayed in the bush all winter and continued trapping until spring. Having lived in that setting, I could easily identify with their way of life.

These days few young people still trap or regularly engage in those pursuits so common in earlier times. Hunting and fishing are common activities for young and old, but the methods here are similar to those employed elsewhere. Still, though some traditions are fading, I have a sense that the native people living within and around Wood Buffalo are still connected to the land, even if it is a tenuous, changing connection. As elsewhere, natives now derive their incomes from a wage economy. Perhaps they can continue to hold their emotional attachments to the land even as their lives become less immediately dependent on it. I hope so because theirs is a land worth protecting, not just for northerners but for humankind.

We broke down our camps and stored all the equipment at the Sweetgrass Cabins. Jeff contacted the park headquarters and made arrangements for a helicopter pickup. We packed up our gear and laid it in the open meadow, then we took a last look at the wilderness. Faintly at first, then increasingly louder the whoop-whoop-whoop of copter blades announced our imminent departure. Within a matter of minutes we were whisked back toward civilization.

We returned the following year, Jeff bringing his family, famed BBC nature films producer Michael Salisbury, and a young assistant, Trent Duchscherer (who in time became my son-in-law). My recollections of those two years on the filming project are etched in my mind. Perhaps it was because Jeff and I had become such a close team. Together we had experienced that intense awareness of a wolf very close to our canoe, answering our howls as if we were another wolf and not humans. Or maybe it's that unforgettable moment when the old bull lunged at me in the field. I suppose the bull's annoyance with me is a symbol of Wood Buffalo. The bull's wildness and my human interference is an ageless cycle. In the end Jeff had successfully captured thousands of feet of images on film. People in thirty countries around the world, in the comfort of dens and living rooms, were able to experience some of the happenings in the delta and to learn some of Wood Buffalo's lessons. I knew they would see it absent the musky smell of bison, the chill of an oncoming storm, the shock of a lunging bison. Yet the film carries something out of the park and into those homes—a sense of what Wood Buffalo is even if not in its entirety. And isn't that all we should be taking from nature—a sense of it rather than its soul?

The buffalo wolf in this system is more than an individual forming part of a bigger population of wolves. It is a link within the system—without that link the system would be very different. No wolves, more bison. More bison, fewer willows and aspen. What keeps the system evolving and changing is the combination of many forces. Natural systems are in a constant condition of flux. Flooding, severity of winter, grasshopper infestation, forest fires, and many other forces shape the system. Linkages are complex and the results are not always predictable. What Jeff, his coworkers, and I experienced was the howl of the predator echoing through time and connected to the past. It will likely continue on for a long time, as long as people allow it to happen. I left that fall with plans to come back in the spring. But this time, alone.

When Scavengers

Become Predators

I was startled by a noise as loud as a musical instrument rhythmically tapping out a beat in the quiet of the wilderness. Where was I? Rousing from a deep sleep, I was momentarily disoriented. I lay still, staring up at the green walls of my fly-camp tent. It took me several seconds to get my mind focused on the sound. It was the tongue of an animal, much like that of a thirsty dog, lapping up water from the creek.

Yes, right. It was spring and I was alone on my first night away from base camp. No film crews along on this trip. Things were much as they were when I first started my work. I was camped along Lynx Stand Creek where a rotten bison carcass rested half submerged along the opposite shore. I was coming out of one of those sound sleeps, with the apprehension that accompanies disorientation. Context returned and I remembered that the day before had been hot and ended late because I had stayed up well into the night watching a wolf pack, the Base Camp Pack, attacking a bison herd. The tapping noise was now familiar—a wolf drinking water, probably after a meal of putrid meat. I stuck my head out between the tent flaps and could see a large gray wolf alone at the water's edge. A breeze blew over the carcass, and I caught the scent of rotting cow.

The cow had most likely broken through the ice in the fall and drowned. Creeks are dangerous places for bison. Spring floods also, when they occurred in earlier years, had taken many a bison's life. Slipping on the ice can result in the splitting of the pelvic girdle. When that happens the bison is paralyzed and dies either a quick death from predators or a slow death from starvation.

I had spotted the carcass in the creek outside my tent a few days before, but slightly upstream. She was floating and appeared intact but was rotting and jellylike. Soon after a bison dies, bacteria take over and reduce the red muscle to a white, viscous mass. The smell is unmistakable. When I spotted the carcass, I thought it unlikely that wolves would get at it because it was too heavy to move to a spot where they could gain a sound footing. My guess was that a black bear in the region would claim it. Bears are usually, but not always, dominant over wolves when the two species arrive at a carcass. So I left the carcass in the creek and went on to do other things. I happened to canoe by the area two days later and was surprised to see that the carcass had been dragged onto shore. The smell cut the air with a stench that was overpowering. Upon my approach I noticed the movement of an animal in the cattails along the bank of the creek and soon recognized it as a wolf. It left when it saw me. Lying in the middle of a large bare area were the remains of the drowned cow. Seeing this I wished I had remained at the site for more detailed observations earlier. Now that my curiosity was piqued, I decided to camp by the carcass to see if scavengers were still interested in the meager remains. I had canoed back to camp, made a cup of tea, had a bowl of soup, returned to the carcass with my small tent, and made myself comfortable for the night.

The wolf crouched for a few minutes and then walked through the emergent vegetation along the creek to the remains of the carcass. It began pulling and tugging at the stinking bones and hide, the putrid smell wafting to where I was. I picked up my binoculars and watched. This was a very large wolf. Its short hair and long legs gave it the appearance of a gray dog. I looked at the animal carefully. How different the wolves look as summer nears. Short summer fur, bedraggled and scruffy, gives the animals much less of a wolflike appearance than in winter. As I watched, the wolf became nervous. Instead of looking my way the wolf was looking in the opposite direction. I soon found out why.

A second wolf appeared. The Base Camp Pack had a rendezvous site nearby, but neither of these wolves belonged to that pack. They got along well together. Both were likely outcasts from the pack. Each intently worked

A pair of wolves scavenge on a carcass, while looking out for the return of the pack.

on some bare bones, going down on their bellies and pulling and tugging at whatever bits of meat, sinew, and hide they could garner. I could see how they used the shearing power of the cheek to tear off strips of sinew.

I watched the wolves feeding on what was left of the carcass and wondered how this pair could possibly have eaten so much over just two days. I soon found the answer to that question. Abruptly the two outcast wolves left, and in about twenty minutes I again saw movement along the emergent vegetation. This time a darker wolf with long black and white guard hair along the back appeared. The animal stopped several times and cautiously looked about, as if sensing some danger. It was a young wolf, and by its size, I judged it to be a female. She was uncanny in both appearance and behavior. There was something very delicate about her whole appearance, highlighted by a snout more pointed than that of most wolves I have seen. I thought it likely she was a hybrid. Wolves and trappers' dogs could meet even in these remote areas and possibly mate. The gentle delta breeze ruffled the hair around the neck and flanks. I named her Lady in Tresses, or Lady for short.

Lady pounced on the rib cage, tugged at it for a few seconds, looking up as if at any moment now she would be struck by some great misfortune. Like a magpie she made a few more quick tugs, then stopped to look around. Nothing. Back to getting a few more scraps. Her movements were quick, erratic, and unsure. I felt sorry for her—what an unfortunate way to exist. This animal appeared to have even less standing than an outcast. About five minutes later the scene changed. Out of the dense clump of willows walked "the Boss"—a large wolf with a steady and deliberate trot, moving through the emergent vegetation to the carcass. This was an alpha animal—medium build but with a massive head. His body language was easy to read. The tail was up in a posture of dominance. As soon as Lady saw him, she bolted. Along with the Boss came a smaller, light-colored wolf—one that I named the Sidekick. These two wolves stayed at the site for thirty-five minutes, with only the Sidekick attempting to get some tidbits from the rotting carcass. The Boss made no attempt to feed. But clearly the carcass was feeding several wolves.

I watched wolves feeding at the bison cow remains for

several hours the next day before I headed back to Base Camp. Scanning the horizon in search of bison, I saw a large herd moving my way. Soon that herd was joined by a second. I took out my scope and, as the animals strung out in a line, estimated their numbers. The first herd consisted of about 100 cows, 10 bulls, 25 calves, and 3 yearlings. The second herd was composed of 40 cows, 5 bulls, 20 calves, and 1 yearling. Numbers are important—the ratios of adult to young are needed to better understand the system. Young born, young surviving, yearling recruitment, these are the data used for predictive models and bison demographics. As the two herds melded together into one unit, I could see the calves of the smaller herd eagerly and playfully nudging each other and apparently picking up the pace in possible anticipation of joining up with the larger herd. For two hours, the herd, now more than 200 animals, grazed in an area around my base camp. Several cows came within a few dozen meters (about 40 feet) of my tent. One wolf returned from its forays on the open delta flats and walked by the herd. The bison gave no sign of alarm as the wolf stopped, looked, perked up its head as if to say "I'll be back later," and walked on. I suspected that if the bison stayed overnight in the area, the wolves would join them near daybreak. I would see my prediction come true the next day.

That evening I thought about the interaction between wolves and bison and was struck by the simplicity of this system. Bison, wolves, live prey, and carcasses. This was truly a food chain as opposed to a more complex food web. I had had experience with a web in earlier studies in

Jasper National Park. The predator-prey dynamic was much more diverse—seven hoofed animals and four large carnivores. In the delta system, wolf predation had a major impact on the demographics of bison. Natives have known that for years. In scientific terms we talk about a "top-down population system." Predators, not habitat or disease, dictate the numbers of bison in the short term. That supported what I had seen, but others placed more emphasis on the impact of diseases. No one who had witnessed the buffalo wolf doing what nature had honed it to do would take that position. Long-term cycles are a different matter.

The next day would bring new insights into the lives of buffalo wolves in this remote wilderness setting. The sun rose at 3:45 but I was up as the light began to break at 3:30. I was awakened by the familiar and pleasing sound of bison. They had chosen my campsite as their grazing turf. Three calves came right up to my tent. It was one of those defining moments—reddish-colored heads, large eyes, and long eyelashes of three buffalo calves only a few paces from my sleeping bag. They looked at me; I looked at them. Then the bison slowly moved on. The mosquitoes were aggressive that morning, buzzing around the screen of the tent door. With one pant leg dragging behind me, I stumbled out of the tent and put on the rest of my clothes. The mosquitoes attacked as soon as I left the security of my screen door. Just as the pink of dawn appeared in the east, I saw the first signs of a new drama between wolves and bison unfolding before me. The large herd had moved to the edge of the willows about five hundred paces from camp. One side of the herd became edgy—at first I thought they were reacting to my clumsy hopping as I tried to put on my pants. That was not the case. The wolves were hunting. Scavengers the previous day, the wolves were now hunters. Through my telescope I could see outlines of three gray shadows bouncing behind the black outlines of the bison. The right flank of the herd gathered speed—a life-and-death struggle was on. In a very tight formation the smaller herd ran out into the open with all the calves in the center. Now I could see four wolves snapping at the heels of the fleeing herd. At 4:05 A.M. the wolves pushed the fleeing herd past my area of vision as they ran some 3 kilometers (1.8 miles) in the open and then veered off past a line of aspen and into an area where I could see neither wolves nor bison.

I started my portable stove and put on a pot of water. The wolves had done exactly what I had expected they would do—attack in the very early hours of the day. Why? Was it visual clues—are the bison disadvantaged? Is it possible the bison are stiff in the early hours of the morning and less likely to gather up momentum in a short period of time? I doubted it, but I was tossing around ideas in my head, grasping for a solution to this conundrum. In any case I was correct in my prediction of the timing. I was beginning to be able to anticipate the buffalo wolf's next moves with some measure of accuracy. This is the basic pattern of science—observe, explain, predict, confirm. It's no different for a lone researcher in the bush trying to unravel the mysteries of natural processes by observing the day-to-day patterns of a predator-prey relationship than it is for a scientist working in a laboratory. Ideally field research should involve more components, such as modern technology and some experimentation. But that is not always possible.

In this instance the pack did come back, as I expected they would, and at the time of day I had surmised. A small prediction, but a sign that I was starting to get it right. I thought about how my skills as a biologist were being tested in the field as opposed to biologists who spend much of their days in front of a computer testing models and composing hypotheses. Probably the greatest difference is that in modeling, a biologist relies on static entities, a set of numbers. In fieldwork the process is multidimensional. Numbers yes, but also intuition and imagination. Imagination is the ability to form mental pictures. For me those pictures are based on previous experiences with bison and wolves. Old sets give rise to new combinations. It is a mixing of knowledge with vision that results in intuitions. I would go about watching, reading signs, and then intuitively conclude that either something took place or anticipate that something might take place. Proof then is either gathered or refuted. It is an amazing process, one denied to those not studying animals and systems up close. It also pointed out to me the importance of long-term research. Understanding of systems requires a cumulative process. The passing of each year, with new insights being added to old ones, superimposed by changing events such as weather cycles, gives a better composite picture of the whole. Short-term studies, no matter how well executed, can never accomplish this. I was reminded of Dick

Dekker, who accomplished remarkable feats by studying avian and mammalian predators over long periods of time at several locations in western Canada. He carried out wolf observations in Jasper National Park after I left and greatly added to our knowledge about that system. As a naturalist and an amateur scientist, Dekker had amassed, over the years, considerable amounts of information about avian and mammalian predators. Unlike other naturalists he also published his findings in peer-reviewed scientific journals. His citation record rivals that of many a professional scientist. I thought about these matters as I sat by my camp.

After a light breakfast I decided to follow the herds, just in case, somewhere in the distance, the wolves had singled out a calf and killed it. I walked about 4 kilometers (2.5 miles) but saw nothing more. The herd had crossed Lousy Creek and that might have discouraged the pack from continuing to press the attack. Although I could not be sure, I considered whether wolf packs disband and re-form, breaking into smaller units that cruise through the area in ones, twos, or threes searching for tidbits—snacks such as lost muskrat, until they re-form to challenge the next herd. This was the basic rhythm of the wolves—resting, scavenging, hunting, killing, resting, the cycle repeating itself again and again. Finding food, whether the red tender flesh of a calf, the tough hide of a beaver, or the rotting flesh of a carcass, is the way wolves spend almost all their energy. And in the search for food, wolves are opportunists.

The large herd that had passed my camp, visited my

tent, and been chased by the pack had evaporated into thin air. The next day I took a cutoff trail to reach a large meadow north of camp. I rounded an old oxbow loop to get to a stand of willow. My attention was drawn to several ravens sitting on the ground, always a sign of wolf activities. Upon examining the area I found the remains of a recently killed calf. Roughly three-quarters of the carcass had been consumed. As I looked up at the other end of the meadow, a cow walked briskly across a clearing and then into an isthmus connecting two adjacent meadows. I knew immediately what the erratic movement of the cow meant. She had lost a calf. Cows will search for many hours, even days, for a lost calf. This strong maternal instinct that is associated with the bonding of mother and young has a chemical basis: oxytocin. Physiological studies by others have determined that. I only saw its consequences.

I knew how to let the cow lead me to where the calf had been killed. A cow will crisscross an area again and again, more or less dissecting the location where the calf was lost. It did not take me long to find the site. Some flattened sedges were the first clue. I bent down to scrutinize the ground and found other clues: small tufts of short reddish hair, a tiny bone fragment, bits of the lower jaw—all that was left of the victim. I gathered all the evidence and it barely covered the palm of my hand. Wolf tracks and scat left no doubt about what had occurred. At least two calves killed at one attack. With due diligence and the help of a single raven, I found small fragments from a third kill. Three calves. Maybe the same ones that a few days earlier had spied into my tent? Any more? Possibly. I could not tell. By then of course the herd was far away, likely to soon again be tested by another hungry pack. When I witnessed such massive intrusion on bison numbers by the wolves, I wondered how the herds could possibly sustain themselves in the system. But they do. Nature's way, one might say, either works or the system destroys itself in the process.

Whether in food chains or in more complicated food webs, the energy stored up in plants is cycled upward into living tissue. A carcass, particularly the size of an adult bison, attracts a host of scavengers, both large and small. Smaller species such as jays, magpies, ravens, weasels, coyotes, and foxes scavenge on bison carcasses. I have watched a red fox chew on meat that was frozen as solid as concrete in midwinter. It ingeniously thawed out a piece of meat by clamping its mouth on it for a time, then stripped the fibers off by pulling at it. Even humans take advantage of bison carcasses. Trappers will seek out frozen carcasses in lakes and rivers. They chop around the frozen bison, tie a rope to the body, and winch it out. The winch is in the form of a pole anchored in ice and twisted to gain the mechanical advantage in the force over distance. Pulley action will haul the carcass onto the surface of the ice. The flesh is then chopped up, loaded onto sleds, and taken home for dog food.

Bears also look to bison carcasses as a source of calories and protein. As with wolves, decomposition is of no consequence to the bears. In fact, rotten carcasses are often relished. I have seen bears wallow in the rotten meat

A black bear sow with young cubs scavenging on the carcass of a bison that had drowned after falling through ice

of the carcass, then proceed to gorge themselves on the remains. Of course having bears and wolves feeding on carcasses means they sometimes meet over an equally coveted meal. Once, along Lousy Creek during spring, I found the skeletal remains of a bear close to that of a bison carcass. The bear skeleton was only 15 meters (50 feet) from that of the bison bones. The animal was a young bear, and I surmised that it was likely killed by a pack of wolves while scavenging on the bison carcass. From evidence left behind, my guess was that this had occurred in the previous fall. I have not seen bears kill bison calves, although I know of five direct interactions between bears and bison in Wood Buffalo. In all cases the behavior of the bears suggested they were trying to prey on calves. That they were trying suggests to me that they are sometimes successful, otherwise the behavior is unlikely to be perpetuated. In two consecutive years, both times during June, Jeff Turner filmed a cinnamon-colored black bear trying to isolate a calf from the herd.

Bears have a much wider range of food preferences than wolves, from beetle larvae to vegetation, carrion to fresh meat, thus they don't depend on bison the way wolves do. When bears and wolves meet at a carcass, it is never a happy encounter, and depending on how many wolves there are, the odds play themselves out. Prevailing wisdom is that bears usually win, but not always. What wolves lack in size they make up for in numbers. Although it might be more common for bears to take over wolf kills, wolves occasionally keep their quarry and have been seen to displace adult bears at carcasses.

Carrion is a valuable source of food within the system. No doubt the presence of bison diseases in the Wood Buffalo herds increases availability of carcasses—so does water in the form of ice. In the park the phenomenon of bison slipping on ice is referred to as "splitters" or "spreaders." Reggie McKay, my best source of information, described what happens in the fall or early winter when there is no snow on clear, or glare, ice.

> The ice is just like a windowpane—you can see through to the bottom; the buffalo get on this and, Mister Man, the

backs slide right out from underneath; something gives. I do not know what—maybe it strains the muscles too much and their backs will give out—that is, once [their legs] spread apart they've had it. They cannot get up. When there is a pack of wolves around, these buggers will come from the back, pull at the rectum and get at the guts—eat the buffalo alive. Cruel bastards—those wolves. We got to get after them, Lu—their fur is good, and you can get a good price for them when they are prime. You know, if you want to get more information on "spreaders," you should check with some other trappers also.

Reggie was being uncharacteristically modest. I did ask others and got much the same information.

A dead cow in a creek, outcasts feeding in the early morning, the arrival of an untouchable hybrid and her quick departure at the arrival of "the Boss," the killing of several calves—all in two days. I knew much more was happening beyond my view, a kaleidoscopic drama in which the characters were constantly adapting to the world around them. I didn't always like the outcome of the drama that I witnessed. Finding the remains of three young calves after a herd peacefully grazed around my tent was, in human terms, a sad ending. But that is nature, red in tooth and claw. Calves struggling against all odds to stay alive in hopeless situations, wolves desperately seeking the next meal to feed whimpering pups back at the den, the bones of a bear telling of how it foolishly misjudged its odds against a pack—these are the realities of life in the wilderness. And these are the same things that attract us to the wild. Perhaps in recognizing their struggles we see a bit of our own long-ago past, the shadow of how we once lived, day by day, meal by meal.

The Fate

of the Herd

Watching bison in Wood Buffalo National Park, with a warming sun tinting the meadows a harvest gold, one can easily forget that the fate of the herd—whether or not to eradicate it—is a constant source of debate. The bison carry diseases that also infect cattle. In the minds of many the solution to disease problems in the bison herds is to eliminate the host. Men and women, often far away, were plotting a strategy to destroy something of which they had little firsthand knowledge. The plan was so extreme in its concept that the media quickly dubbed it the "Armageddon option."

To me, nothing symbolizes lack of human insight about the Wood Buffalo ecosystem better than a letter published in Canada's premier newspaper, the *Globe and Mail*. The writer suggested that "as a result of disease the park herd will have died out in less than 10 years." Written in 1990, that essentially meant no more bison in the park by the year 2000. By 2002 the herd was not only flourishing but also increasing. This letter stands out in my mind as a milestone because it was written by a powerful voice on such an issue, Canada's director of animal health. No one doubted his sincerity, but one needed to question his bona fides—how could he be so sure and where did he get these insights? The official went on to say that "all free roaming bison in northwestern Canada will probably die." In the background was always the issue of cattle and dreams of a disease-free cattle herd for all of Canada. The bison of Wood Buffalo were in the way.

In August of that same year a federal government review panel agreed with the director of animal health and recommended slaughtering the entire herd. The main purpose of the proposed program was to address the disease issues, but lesser agendas included restoring the wood bison "purity" and providing the opportunity for human hunting of bison, once a herd had reached the carrying capacity of its range. Things were looking bleak for the bison of Wood Buffalo. Powerful forces, some well intentioned, had them in their sights. Extermination and replacement of the bison with a "disease-free" herd from elsewhere were laid out as the only prudent steps. Coming from people with responsibility and power, the statement caught the attention of more than a few; in fact, some eleven thousand letters worldwide were sent in opposition to these draconian plans. Had the plans been carried out, it would have meant that the last continuous dance between bison and wolves in North America would have come to an end. It also would have meant the destruction of a genetic base that later was considered valuable and worth saving. Proof of that occurred when an official genetic salvaging plan was carried out for the nearby Slave River Lowlands population. This program was instituted in anticipation of a large-scale management effort for the region.

The bison needed an ally. They found one in the northern natives living around the park, legally known as the Treaty Eight Indians. Their technical advisers read the report and bluntly labeled it "scientific bullshit." Nevertheless the federal panel rejected any scientific arguments for protecting the herd. Arguments for depopulation prevailed. Those who wanted to protect disease-free herds from contamination scored important points. Actions were needed to prevent the spread of diseases from the park to the Mackenzie bison herds. However, there were many other agendas, some hidden, others open. One was the genetic question. "Hybrid" bison in Wood Buffalo National Park were to be replaced by "pure" wood bison. Groups such as the Wood Bison Recovery Team wanted a disease- and hybrid-free environment for biological restoration of "pure wood bison." In reality a large free-roaming prairie bison herd, the Pink Mountain herd, is close enough to Wood Buffalo that the exchange of genes is always a possibility. Not to mention the many captive-game ranching operations using plains bison throughout the north. Escapes and mingling with free-ranging buffalo are possibilities in bison ranching. So the future flow of genes from prairie bison to wood bison had at least two routes. As far as I was concerned "purity" was unachievable.

Native communities in the north were wholly unimpressed by the panel's recommendations. They made their opinion known at hearings and through media interviews. Chief Pat Marcel of the Fort Chipewyan band put it this way, "It's more evidence of the arrogance of the federal government pushing their agenda on us. It's not acceptable anymore." Others from a northern Alberta Indian tribe put it in even starker terms: "Any act against the buffalo will be regarded as an act of hostility against the tribe." Employees from Parks Canada too were furious. Here were people who watched the herds, regularly counted them, and saw through the phoniness of some of the rhetoric. They were officially muzzled, but unofficially and behind closed doors they formed a coalition, calling themselves BERT (the Bison Emergency Rescue Team). Officials in Ottawa were concerned about the in-house resistance and sent a deputy minister to investigate. Fortunately the superintendent of the park protected his employees and nothing came of it. They kept their jobs.

Like many other biologists, I found myself embroiled in a political debate with serious ecological and social consequences. I did not categorically rule out any of the options, including depopulation. The reason for this was simple—a scientist should look at the facts and always keep an open mind. But what I saw in the bush and what was discussed at the hearings simply did not add up.

Therefore, I took an opposing view from that of the federal panel and of many of my peers. I could not agree with the well-intentioned but often inexperienced people whose analysis of the problems was garnered from the rhetoric of those who came to the table with agendas. Nor could I agree with those whose views were predicated only on pragmatic thinking in "hard science." I believe studies of animals in a natural setting can never be equated to the physical sciences. There are too many variables. Regression lines and statistics were supposed to demonstrate the hard, scientific facts. Maybe on paper, but not in the dynamics of the ecosystems involved. A decrease in recent bison numbers was predicted in the regression lines of many models, and statisticians looked confused when they saw the results of surveys years later. I was not surprised. Above all, I objected to the cavalier attitude that science was unimportant, as if to say "we do not need any research; the facts (declines) are obvious."

To understand the parts, one needs to look at the whole. The great scientist and naturalist Alexander von Humboldt was one of the first to make that assertion. Few were willing to do that in the Wood Bison National Park debate. Many came to the table with an agenda. They grasped at facts, strong or weak, to support their positions. Looking at the whole meant being open minded. What we already know can sometimes prevent us from accepting new ideas. That diseases were entrenched in the herds was well known. But what are the implications in evolutionary terms? Could hosts develop some degree of immunity toward these pathogens? Was depopulation the only or even the best solution to this perplexing problem? I did not think so. I had observed the wolves, the bison, the ecosystem in which they lived, and their interactions one with the other. It is not a perfect system—to be sure. But evolution is molding its components into a workable unit. In my view more in-depth research was the answer. It was not just a matter of carrying out a study, but of putting science into its rightful place in the first instance. That called for an integrated, multidisciplinary program, not a narrowly focused three-year project. I believed that when more information was available the whole issue would be revisited. My maxim was, "Never rule out options, but get your information first."

Few of the facts I saw in 1990 convinced me of the urgency to jump headlong into a depopulation effort. Proponents for the depopulation plan kept pushing regression lines under my nose—lines that predicted the bison would die out. "See, here is evidence—this herd is doomed! It is down, down, down and will soon be gone." Disease, they said, is the only reason the herd is declining. Obviously they had never watched a buffalo wolf in the wild. You just had to walk the buffalo trails in spring and see that most of the wolf scats had fine rusty orange hair in them to consider that disease was not the only cause for bison deaths. Bison calves are regularly killed at an early age, and those that survive are tested throughout their lives. I was convinced that predation, not disease, kept bison numbers down. Others contended, and I agreed, that even if the wolves remained, bison numbers might well increase if you removed the diseases.

The debate is about proximate and ultimate factors. Without cattle diseases that influence calf production, bison numbers may increase to levels at which predation eliminates fewer individuals than the numbers that are born into the population. That would put the herds in a positive growth phase until overpopulation reaches new critical levels. Could starvation be one possibility, once there are too many bison? The ecological picture is complex, but positions taken by different schools of thought were entrenched and that bothered me a great deal. There was little tolerance for other opinions; if you did not agree with someone else's idea, not uncommonly the approach was simply to ignore it and shove it under the proverbial carpet.

Scientists bent on killing the bison began showing photographs of weak, diseased, and crippled bison as evidence of the hideous nature of the diseases. They were playing on the emotions of the public. Other scientists, bent on saving the herds, were doing the same—showing photographs of bison that looked healthy and vigorous. Slaughter proponents would have the public believe that the bison were a pathetic lot of dying animals. It was a charade and I was a part of the whole frenzied event. Friends of long standing would glare at me from across a table, armed with facts to support their positions. Many a phone call descended into heated, caustic debate. Park wardens from different national parks would argue different sides of the issue. If you worked in Wood Buffalo National Park, you wanted to protect the herds; if you worked in Elk Island National Park, you wanted the depopulation program so that you could transfer Elk

Island bison, disease free and "pure," back into the north country. Facts were marshaled to support each opinion.

So how was it that the population ended up being targeted for extermination? How could Wood Buffalo National Park be proclaimed a World Heritage site for "protecting the largest free-roaming bison left in existence" in 1983 and be the target for massive depopulation of bison herds seventeen years later? An assessment of events tells us much about conservation, wildlife science, agricultural-wildlife conflicts, and, indeed, human nature. It is hard for one's professional background not to influence one's personal perspective. I am no exception. For example, upon hearing from a warden at Wood Buffalo that the latest census showed an increase in bison numbers, I shouted with glee. My predictions were being supported by unfolding events. Keep your useless regression lines! Not very scientific, more emotional than logical. I too was playing a numbers game. The information on the increase simply refuted many of the arguments and predictions others had made earlier in the decade.

Counting animals is critical, but it is only one stage in a process that should include getting answers to the whys and the hows. Those answers come from looking at connections, evaluating environmental conditions, and piecing together the components that drive the system. The Wood Buffalo herd has a history connected to human manipulation. We know little about the herds before 1900, but we do have bits and pieces recorded by explorers and trappers. The first European to discover the northern buffalo was Samuel Hearne. On his way from the subarctic he and his team crossed Great Slave Lake in January 1772. His team began their trek up the east side of the Slave River and encountered "Buffalo, moose and beaver." Hearne was struck by the size of the bison, writing: "the Buffalo in those parts, I think are generally much larger than the English black cattle—in fact they are so heavy, that when 6 to 8 Indians are in company at the skinning of a large bull, they never attempt to turn it over while entire, but when the upper side is skinned, they cut off the leg and shoulder, rip open the belly, take out all the intestines, cut off the head, and make it as light as possible, before they turn it to skin the under side."

The New World bison massacres of the nineteenth century reduced the great herds to a shadow of what they once were. At the same time, wolf killing was considered a duty. In most places the bison and the wolves were both gone; in a few places the bison alone remained; other areas had wolves but no bison. Only in the remote northeast corner of Alberta, that place later named Wood Buffalo National Park, did both remain together in the same ecosystem. Yet the Wood Buffalo bison did not entirely escape civilization's reach. Scraps of historical records suggest that at the end of the nineteenth century bison numbers were low in the region due in part to extensive hunting. By the turn of the century governments in both the United States and Canada began to see bison as national treasures. In the early twentieth century the Canadian government purchased the largest plains bison herd then in existence from a rancher named Michel Pablo and transferred it to an area near Wainright, Alberta. Those animals, with a few others mixed in, had originated from six motherless calves, the last survivors of the Blackfoot Indian hunt in Montana, which had followed Samuel Walking Coyote's horses back to camp. It was a remarkable story that such a magnificent prairie mammal, so close to extinction, was able to make a comeback. For Canadians, what sounded like good news turned out to have a downside. The herd, in its newly acquired sanctuary near Wainwright, was soon overpopulated. The bison managers decided to "help" the bison in Wood Buffalo. Bison from the south were moved to the north. Between 1925 and 1928 a massive effort took place to bring plains bison to Wood Buffalo. Genetic considerations aside, plains bison from the south had been exposed to cattle, and today those bison are the prime suspects in the introduction of tuberculosis and brucellosis. Having spent so much effort moving the bison north, few involved wanted to see them eaten by wolves. So wolf control programs began in the 1930s, picking up pace in the 1940s when reports of wolves slaughtering bison surfaced. Dewey Soper, a biologist and naturalist, was pushing for wolf control.

Soper first conducted fieldwork in Wood Buffalo National Park in the spring of 1932, and in a 1945 report for the Canadian Wildlife Service, he stated that the work "was pursued almost incessantly at all seasons of the year until early spring 1934." He traveled by dog team and boat and covered most of the region from the vicinity of Birch Mountain north to the Nyarling River and Great Slave Lake, west to Buffalo Lake, the upper waters of Buffalo and Little Buffalo Rivers, Thultue Lake, and the Jackfish River drainage. Shorter trips were made in the park in 1937, 1939, and 1944, with more detailed investigations in 1945. Soper's trips to the park in the 1930s were focused on general faunal investigations, with some specific studies dealing with the status and life history of bison. A lengthy monograph on bison published in *Ecological Monographs* resulted from that work. Soper's official instructions in 1945 were to study the interrelationships of timber wolves and bison. "Report on Wildlife Investigations" was written upon his return from the field. The report dealt at length with wolf predation on bison. He concluded that the predator was too numerous and posed a real threat to the bison herds.

> [H]aving correctly reached the conclusion that wolves are everywhere on the increase across the North and that it is desirable to reduce their numbers for certain specific and justifiable reasons, the fundamental objective, then, is to get rid of a goodly percentage of them. At the moment nothing else matters. It is a question of killing wolves. No other issue should obscure this proposition. . . . [T]hree dead wolves are better than none and the three are dead, incontestably dead. They are beyond the powers of reproduction and destruction. If we want to kill wolves, does it much matter, within reason, how they become defunct? The point as I see it under the circumstances is to momentarily set aside some of the disputations of the situation and go straight to the objective—reduction of the wolf population. The answer is comparatively simple—"kill them."

Two decades after the introduction of plains bison into the park, and more than a decade after wolf control was initiated, the first aerial surveys were undertaken. As summarized in *Wolves, Bison* by Carbyn, Oosenbrug, and Anions, the 1947 bison survey covered about 30 percent of the park and provided an estimate of 7,500 bison for the entire park—likely a conservative estimate based on the sampling protocol. Two years later, Bill Fuller conducted an aerial survey and estimated that Wood Buffalo had about 12,500 bison. In a 1951 survey Fuller came to the conclusion that the population level was similar to that of his 1949 survey.

In the 1950s and up until the late 1960s wolf control was still in its heyday, but park personnel embraced the idea of intensive bison management as well. These were years of rounding up bison and slaughtering hundreds for disease testing and prevention, attempts to control tuberculosis and anthrax. In the end the efforts did little to control the diseases or for that matter to reduce the infection rates. But with fewer wolves, the herds nonetheless prospered. By the late 1960s killing wolves became unpopular, and both the official and unofficial wolf control programs ceased. Then in 1968 the Bennett Dam on the Peace River was completed, something that may have initiated subtle and not-so-subtle changes in the delta ecosystem, though the causes of ecological change are complex and difficult to assess. Bison surveys by park wardens became more regular and more reliable, providing estimates that scientists found credible. In 1970 the surveys found that the bison in Wood Buffalo numbered approximately 11,000. By 1994 the number had fallen to only 2,300, but soon the bison population stabilized at 2,500. By 2002 the numbers had increased considerably. Short lived? Possibly. What increases can also decrease. Proponents of depopulation heralded the 80 percent population decrease since the 1970s as evidence that diseases were causing the decline. Some blamed the drying of the delta; some argued it was predation; still others pointed to all three causes.

What really happened? No one has all the answers; almost everyone has an opinion, as do I. First, I don't put much stock in blaming disease. The single most important piece of evidence exonerating disease is the state of the herd before 1970. The park's bison had been infected with disease since 1925, yet the number of bison in the 1930s, 1940s, and 1950s was high and stable or growing, depending on how you interpret the surveys. I saw nothing fundamentally different about diseases in the park before 1970 and after 1970, hence my reluctance to blame disease for the decrease in bison population. In a way, the presence of disease in the Wood Buffalo bison population is a sign of the strength of the herd. They have been saddled with diseases, droughts, fires, floods, predators, and changes in food supplies and climate, yet they continue to survive.

When the wolves were diminished, the prey in this simple food chain flourished. When wolf control ended and their numbers blossomed, the bison population was brought back down to lower numbers. Of course disease probably does make it easier for wolves to kill bison. And diseases have other impacts—affecting reproduction and longevity. Weakened by disease, the herd was probably more susceptible to predation. Years of watching wolves and bison gave me some confidence when I voiced my opinion that the herd was far more likely to survive into the twenty-first century than to disappear. To me, wolves seemed to account for most of the bison declines seen in the 1970s and 1980s as well as the later stabilization and subsequent small increases in bison numbers. It's a matter of fitting together the pieces of the puzzle. More wolves, fewer bison—fewer bison, fewer wolves; the numbers vary up and down.

I felt I had it pretty well worked out and still do. But those who supported eradication pointed not to wolves as the source of the bison's decline but to diseases. Still others thought the decline was the result of the construction of Bennett Dam, which they believed had altered the delta ecosystem for the worse. To complicate matters further, in the 1970s the northwestern areas of Canada entered a long-term drought cycle. Whether due largely to the drought, the dam, or a combination of factors, the delta began to dry up. Disease, drought, a dam, and cessation of wolf control all affect the fabric of a complex ecosystem. And the dry delta (an oxymoron) of the 1980s and early 1990s was certainly quite different from the delta I had first come to know. So I believed that a program directed at restoration of water levels in the delta would be more important than killing the bison. Ecosystem restoration, like building a house, should start with the foundation, no with the roof.

By the time I had worked out the biological interaction between bison declines and wolf predation to my satisfaction, the political process was just beginning to heat up again. It was widely accepted that the Wood Buffalo bison population was not a viable population—soon it would crash close to zero (or very low numbers, depending on to whom you talked), the end, extinction. It was considered a diseased population that needed to be replaced, a population ready to be tossed on the garbage dump of history. Waiting in the wings, we were told, were disease-free bison, vigorous, healthy, and aesthetically pleasing. And these were pure wood bison, not some wood bison with seventy-five-year-old plains bison DNA mixed in. They could be readily transported from other parks, taking the place of Wood Buffalo's "lepers" of the bison world. Indeed, didn't Wood Buffalo, for the sake of its name if nothing else, deserve to have clean, pure wood bison? The debate focused on the "pure" and the "defiled." Lined up on the side of the pure were the ranchers, members of the agricultural industry, some academics, and the World Wildlife Fund, to name a few. Lined up on the side of the defiled were the native communities of the north, Parks Canada, other academics, and the Canadian Nature Federation. Round one went to the defiled—the government decided it needed more time before slaughtering the herd.

The coalition of purists was composed of those who were concerned with cattle economics and some conservationists who wanted to see the herd return to a disease-free and genetically pristine state. Biology, like politics, creates strange bedfellows, as was the case when the cattlemen's association courted World Wildlife Fund officials who wanted "purity" in wood bison genetics. In essence, the conservation purists wanted bison to return to the way they imagined they were in pre-Columbian times. Over time, studies cast substantial doubt on the issue of genetics. There may be some slight genetic differences between wood and plains bison, but scientists were having a hard time finding them. It was looking more and more like genetic purity was going to be a hard sell. That left the conservation purists with elimination of disease as their main selling point. Basically they argued that the herd was a risk to itself and to other bison; the cattle interests were quite concerned about the health of their own herds, which at least occasionally encountered wild bison.

I don't dispute the points set forth by the cattle ranchers. It seems to me only honest to admit that, in the short run, there are sound economic reasons for killing all the bison in Wood Buffalo. With bison gone, the brucellosis and tuberculosis would probably decline substantially for a time, and the cattle herds would be less at risk for some number of years. But who is to say that ten, fifty, or a hundred years from now we would not again be faced with the same problems? Tuberculosis, for example, surfaces in areas where it was thought to have been eliminated. It is also unrealistic to think that eliminating two diseases creates disease-free environments.

Even the best-case scenario, total elimination of brucellosis and tuberculosis, leaves a third and highly infectious disease in Wood Buffalo—anthrax. Anthrax spores are in the soil, and as the world has learned after the deplorable anthrax mailings in the United States, this is a hard disease to eliminate. Indeed, it's likely that nothing can ever be done to rid Wood Buffalo of anthrax. It seemed that if the slaughter was allowed to proceed, the most compelling experts could offer no guarantee that the replacement herd would be disease free—for all times.

Edmonton

Rush hour in modern cities is much the same around the world. Cars, traffic lights, people. Edmonton, Alberta, Canada, is no exception. It was March 2001, and my mind wandered north to Wood Buffalo National Park as I drove through downtown along Jasper Avenue. Edmonton, a city of about seven hundred thousand people, is known as the gateway to Canada's north, lying some 650 kilometers (400 miles) south of the Peace-Athabasca Delta and Wood Buffalo National Park.

I was on my way to meetings in one of the posh downtown hotels. Parks Canada, once again, was hosting a forum to talk about bison and diseases. Officially, this was to be the last meeting of the Research Advisory Committee, a group of representatives from native communities, cattle interests, the scientific community, and some conservation groups. I wasn't on the committee but had been invited to see the results of their work. I tried to be hopeful, but I was worried about a research committee so packed with nonresearchers. I hoped for something akin to the bison research workshop held for Yellowstone National Park under the able leadership of François Messier and Bill Gasaway. I was soon to learn that the Research Advisory Committee was more political than scientific in nature.

As I entered the lobby of the hotel, I thought about what these next few days might bring. The specific purpose of the three-day meeting, I had been told, was to provide a forum in which Canadian and U.S. researchers, managers, and representatives could exchange and discuss ideas. The focus of the meeting was the recently completed study on diseases of bison in Wood Buffalo National Park. In some respects the study was well executed, but it had its critics. My main concern was the narrowness of its focus—why spend all available resources only on disease-related issues? Some important factors were completely overlooked. For example, during the three-year direction of the study, much of the delta had been flooded. The floods destroyed many of the wolf dens. This likely had a major impact on bison mortality, yet the events went unrecorded. Why? Another criticism was that it used manipulative, highly invasive techniques such as "net gunning" bison from the air and placing bison in small cages to test for disease prevalence. I wondered why darting from the ground was not used. When I asked, I was told, "one could not possibly get close enough." When I told them it was possible to get within feet of bison, I was met with looks of disbelief. Cost too was an issue. Of the $4–5 million allocated, only about $1.6 million was applied to the study itself. Had funds been directed to a broader approach, much more would have been learned about the unique ecosystem. If readers are interested in more specifics on costs, they are directed to Carbyn and Watson, 2001. But the biggest problem I had with the study had to do with the interpretation of its results. In an article in the *Edmonton Journal,* the chief biologist in charge of the multimillion-dollar study reported that "49 percent of the bison in the park are infected with tuberculosis and 31 percent with brucellosis." "If nothing is done," the story continued, "the herd will likely drop to as low as 1,000 animals." Big news, scary news. It made the headlines, but I had grave doubts about its accuracy.

The meeting facilitator introduced members of the committee and passed out folders. I opened mine up and looked at the list of attendees. The native representation was strong—twenty-six individuals from a number of northern communities. Later that evening, in the quiet of my study, I had a closer look at the list. In addition to the twenty-six native representatives were twenty scientists, eight delegates from agriculture, and only two from conservation groups. I was struck by the high caliber of U.S. veterinarians and pathologists but also concerned that there wasn't a diversity of scientific views. Disease control advocates were heavily represented. I was on the outside looking in, and what I saw concerned me.

The morning of the next day started on a subdued and

somber note. The facilitator advised scientists to discuss science and to leave management plans for another day. The opening statements by federal and provincial officials were not memorable, simply what one would expect from agency representatives. One biologist took the stage and excitedly began to describe how management should be carried out. He was reminded that this was a research-oriented meeting. Management, we were told, falls into a different realm. That would be up to the responsible agencies whose mandate it is to manage the resources. The task ahead was to evaluate the results of the recently completed study.

Then the native representatives spoke up. Things became more lively. Though this was supposedly a meeting to deal with science and research initiatives, not a political rally, political rhetoric soon dominated the room. I was surprised to learn that most of the native representatives seemed to be in favor of the depopulation option. Ten years ago the natives had fought the proposed management program, the so-called Armageddon option; now they seemed to support it. The most politicized speeches of all came from the representatives of a small community north of the park. But some of the scientific papers were also strongly agenda driven; biased views were supported by unbiased data. Any scientific meeting, I thought, would put far more caveats on the sweeping generalizations that were being made.

As I looked about, it seemed that proponents of depopulation were delighted with what they were hearing. The "natives will have no problem getting rid of every last buffalo"—"just look," we were told, "at the [Wood Buffalo] border situation now—bison on one side of the border and skidoo tracks and no bison on the other side." The inference was clear: any bison that exited the park were quickly dispatched. Another native representative echoed similar sentiments: "Just give us the bucks; we know how to do the job for you!" What a change. These were natives with a view different from those who had lobbied to protect the herds a decade before. Even in the washroom the buzz was loud. I heard a native representative lobbying the Ottawa Parks Canada delegate: "Tell your minister to give us 100 million dollars to clean up the disease mess." Politicians and biologists in favor of slaughtering bison were comrades-in-arms. They chatted about how much fun they had boating into the delta together.

During the coffee break I touched base with a biologist from Ottawa. He was distressed. Here he was, a senior biologist for Parks Canada who needed to get information to write up a briefing paper for the minister. He looked at me. "What should I tell the minister—millions of dollars spent on the project and all we get is this?" He had read my mind. "Where is the science? Where are the facts on the bigger picture?" What a dilemma for Parks Canada. The biologist was alarmed. This he said was "poor science." I felt for him. The burden of responsibility weighed heavily on his shoulders. On the second day of the meeting I saw him sprawled on the floor along the aisle with extreme back pain but still speaking up on various issues.

I chatted with another biologist whose reputation as a scientist I respected. I had known him for years and had served on a number of professional societies with him. But at these meetings he represented a different political master and it showed. He came with an agenda—that of the provincial government. Kill the Wood Buffalo bison was his view. He liked what he heard. Good data, he said. This, he asserted, should put pressure on Parks Canada to clean up their act. I dragged myself out of the meetings, dejected, crestfallen. How could the natives have changed their views so drastically from those of ten years ago? "Any act against the buffalo will be regarded as an act against the tribe" still rang in my ears. I went outside. I needed time; I needed space. Conclusions supported by facts seemed to be completely superfluous. The science presented at this meeting was agenda driven. Then I began to wonder just how representative these vocal proponents of annihilation were. Were there other voices not represented at this meeting? Or voices here that had not yet been heard? Scientists who questioned the merits of "depopulation" in past years had not been invited. Why?

The next day the tone of these "research-oriented meetings" really heated up. A well-presented technical paper set the tone. Diseases in free-roaming bison were about to cross the line and infect free-roaming, disease-free bison, namely those in the Hay-Zama Lake area. That was a frightening prospect. If true, it would require immediate attention. But nothing heard to that point had a greater impact on the workshop than the fiery speech of a northern politician. A lean young man, he spoke with great fluency. If you closed your eyes, you could hear the eloquent speeches of chiefs telling the Indian nations of bygone days about the injustices of the white man coming to take over their lands, their hunting grounds, and their bison. This young man was well aware of his gift for oratory. With a grandiloquent wave of his hand, he introduced the thirteen other people from his community—young and old, leaders and followers. "We support the need to know," he said, "but we want action; we need finality to the disease question. We are appreciative of all the smart and good work done so far—but it is not yet finished. More money is needed to get the job done." He reminded the audience that his people were Treaty Eight subjects, with promises from the queen (Queen Victoria), and if need be they would use the legal system to get rid of diseased bison. At this point I watched the face of the Parks Canada representative. His minister would be receiving the brunt of the pressure. Either way, the minister loses—he will get headlines for opposing the natives or for killing thousands of bison in a national park. The politician figuratively patted the audience on the back: "We do not have a problem with any of you folks; we have a problem with those above you."

This was it. Support for the depopulation option was mounting. I didn't see how it could be stopped. Parks Canada had not set the stage for a balanced debate. The audience was being both rallied and threatened. The herds had three strikes against them—native pressure for economic gains, agricultural pressure for disease-free cattle, and conservation pressure for genetic purity. There was no underground support from Parks Canada this time—people from the Bison Emergency Rescue Team had dispersed and were scattered across the country. New employees at

Wood Buffalo appeared to be less committed to saving the bison. At the next break I felt isolated, as if I were the only one who was opposed to Operation Armageddon without a proper review of the facts. This whole meeting lacked balance. Maybe I should just leave, I thought, and get on with other matters.

Sitting in front, all through the sessions, were three people. One was a native from northern Alberta, a quiet, shy mystic. Another was a young blond woman, a student from Europe conducting research on traditional knowledge and native studies. The third was a trapper, the brother of the mystic. The mystic was given the floor. The young woman and the trapper joined him on stage. The mystic was a middle-aged man, slightly stooped, casting his glance downward, avoiding eye contact whenever possible. The woman introduced him as a man still closely tied to the land, who had watched southern values infiltrate his domain, who was upset by trophy hunters killing bison in his area, bison from the Wood Buffalo National Park region. Then the trapper took the microphone. He spoke in a low, soft voice as if he were talking to himself—despite the microphone only inches from his mouth, the audience strained to hear him. He spoke softly, with emotional pauses, his body language conveying his inner conviction. He told of how the bison accepted him, of how they listened to him when he talked to them—then the longest pause, the audience was spellbound—he spoke of the white cloud circling through the bush settling among the herd.

This is not the stuff of modern science. Here was a chapter from the past—a deep, spiritual connection to the land. This man had retained his roots—no amount of money could loosen his ties to the land. Perhaps the fate of the Wood Buffalo bison was not yet sealed. Maybe, just maybe, native values were not so tightly bound to the material worth of the modern world. I could not help but think back to an earlier comment from a politician. "We got a bunch of diseased animals in Wood Buffalo National Park that we got to clean up—man introduced this problem and it should be man that cleans up this mess—we cannot do it overnight. If we get clean animals we can get tourists into the park—ten to fourteen years from now we would have a healthy herd for the tourists." My sentiments were with the trapper—not the politician. The trapper and I had seen the buffalo wolf in action, had seen the bison herds in their natural habitat. And soon science would reenter the picture.

The wardens service was completing its surveys of the Wood Buffalo bison herd as the meeting was taking place. In a few weeks the news would reach everyone in attendance—the surveys showed an increase in the herds from a low of 2,400 bison to 3,200. The next year, the surveys indicated an increase to 4,000 bison. A year later, when the warden in charge of the surveys presented these results to the Wood Bison Recovery Team, team members were disheartened to learn that bison numbers were increasing. This is probably the first time a recovery team, whose responsibility it is to save threatened or endangered species, has been disappointed in such encouraging news. I had already noted that wolf numbers were down from former years. Without wolves or even with few wolves in the system, bison numbers would predictably increase to their former level of 12,000 or more, in stark contrast to the prediction in the *Edmonton Journal* that "the herd will likely drop to as low as 1,000 animals." The system is dynamic. By the year 2003 reports of large packs of wolves were again common. The logical consequence of an increase in wolves is that prey numbers will decline, proof, I believe, that the buffalo wolf, not disease, drives the system.

The Edmonton meetings resolved nothing. I suggested that the process of studying the delta system continue. Funds, it was concluded, were not available. Debates over the future of the herd continue. For my part, I have developed an abiding fondness for these outcasts, these "diseased hybrids." I have watched them survive against great odds—floods, disease, drought, predators, fire. They continue to fare far better than their detractors give them credit for. As a scientist I believe it is unwise to repeat the useless—even counterproductive—interventions wrought unto their numbers in the past. Certainly not without a more comprehensive understanding of the ecosystem in which they live. Far better to be prudent rather than rash and to avoid repeating past mistakes. Some other scientists agree. So do many of the natives who are still attached to the land. Only 150 years ago aboriginal North Americans complained about the white man killing the buffalo. If the soft-spoken trapper has his way—and he might—then the bison and the buffalo wolf in Wood Buffalo National Park will still have a fighting chance.

A Silent Spring

After the Edmonton meetings, I found myself in the company of a small group of wilderness enthusiasts and adventurers, and Brad Burke, a local outfitter. I was entering a new phase in my relationship with the delta. Peter Jonker, from the University of Saskatchewan, had asked me to become involved with a program to bring wilderness education to those who wanted to learn more about this unique area. I had worked with him on two other occasions and the experience had been worthwhile. So I signed on for this ten-day trip. Gone was the intensity associated with data gathering. This was more relaxed, and whatever insights I gathered were more experiential and observational. It was a new challenge to show groups of

Reminders of bison slaughters from the 1950s and 1960s

people Wood Buffalo firsthand. I couldn't guarantee a close encounter with bison and wolves, but at least I could show them the "arena" of their battles.

We were heading down the familiar trail between Sweetgrass Landing and Sweetgrass Cabins. Water levels in the delta were too low to access the lower end of the delta so we approached the site from the north. It was a beautiful, bright, sunny day, and our search image was for the elusive buffalo wolf. So far, none were in sight, but we had not yet reached the open meadows. The path from Sweetgrass Landing to the cabins had not changed much since I first walked it. The trail had been a major transportation corridor used in the 1950s and 1960s by construction workers to build and maintain corrals for slaughtering bison. Nature had healed the scars on the soil, and it now felt like a comfortable, even quaint, game trail. Other signs of human activity were fading as well—the dirt road that once connected a flourishing sawmill site on the banks of the Peace River; the bustling bison processing plant at Sweetgrass Station; the bulldozers, trucks, and vehicles that carried supplies and people to the corrals—they were ghosts of a time past. The road, once a transportation corridor for heavy-duty equipment, was now a footpath, bordered by greenery and signed with the tracks of wildlife.

It occurred to me that much like the trail, the whole ecosystem had undergone a healing process. Where once the interplay of wolves and bison had been destroyed by predator control programs, it now had a chance to continue. Where once humans felt the need to micromanage nature by slaughtering bison for meat production and disease control, there was now the beginning of a return to a more pristine world. The kind of world that prevailed in earlier times. Then something struck me as odd. As I scanned the fresh mud on the trail, I saw no wolf tracks. Where was the fresh scat with bison calf hair in it? My companions were not aware of this change; they had no yardstick by which to measure its loss. Nor did we hear a single howl, not the distant howling of a pack or the call of the lone wolf. From a carnivore's perspective, it was a silent spring. I was here to experience wolves—my wolves, my companions for many years in this country—but they were not here.

For my guests, identifying 125 bird species and sighting black bears, foxes, deer, and moose seemed to make up for the lack of dramatic wolf encounters they had anticipated. We spotted more white-tailed deer in those ten days than

I had seen in all the previous twenty-three years combined. No wolves, more deer. No wolves, bison numbers up. A coincidence? Possibly. I could offer no clear explanation when questioned by my fellow travelers as days passed without the promised wolves. Even if the wolf population had declined in response to a reduction in bison, I had not expected them to be this scarce. I shrugged my shoulders and muttered, "I don't know."

As the trip went on I continued to be preoccupied with the question of why the wolves seemed to be absent from the area in which we traveled. There could be any number of causes, and my speculations on the subject would only skim the surface—probably missing the real answer. Yet I couldn't help wondering. Perhaps a turnover of alpha wolf pack members? Or maybe the packs had moved their denning activities to other locations? Could diseases have reduced wolf numbers? Had the wolves just shifted to new areas as prey became scarce? While speculating about these possibilities, I had to remind myself that ten days is a very small window. Yet it was enough to make a comparison and conclude that something was different in my study area.

As the trip was nearing its end, we camped along the south shore of the Peace River. I was about to settle in for the night when I heard the unmistakable grunting of cows with calves traveling in a herd. I unzipped my tent door and dashed out to the edge of the river to investigate. I watched as events unfolded on the other side of the river. Soon I was joined by the rest of the camp. Thirty bison plunged over a steep bank into the swollen water of the Peace River.

The herd was crossing the river and swimming in our direction. The bison were headed for what appeared to be an exit point along the south side of the river. There was only one such exit out of the river channel and it was blocked by our small boat, which we had used to cross the river. Normally that would not have been a problem. The sandbar along the water's edge usually allows for easy footing for any four-legged animal on the river. But this was May, a time of year when the water had risen considerably. Consequently the water was high above the sandbars, and the bison faced steep banks and the fast-moving current along the river's edge. The banks of the river dropped off 2 to 5 meters (6.5 to 16 feet), forming a formidable obstacle. We climbed down the bank to move the boat, but by the time we got it dislodged, the bison had swum past us and were heading downstream.

Feeling helpless, we watched as the herd kept swimming in circles, looking for a way out of the dilemma. They were unable or unwilling to swim upstream and return to the passageway we had cleared. For more than an hour and a half we watched, and we feared for the lives of that hapless herd of cows, calves, and bulls. Huge uprooted tree trunks floated at considerable speed toward the herd, threatening to bowl the bobbing heads under, where the undertow might claim its victims. The herd drifted downstream then headed against the current, briefly circling, trying desperately to get out on the south shore. I felt certain they had been chased into the river by wolves from the north. The herd seemed ready to risk drowning rather than return to the north shore.

I marveled at the toughness of these animals. Endurance, persistence, and stamina—the drive to overcome all odds was remarkable. Tenacity paid off. An adult cow found a wedge in the bank, secured her footing, and led the herd to safety. The whole herd followed and disappeared out of our sight into the forest cover. We all felt an overwhelming sense of relief, as if we ourselves had escaped the rapids.

I had seen enough; I decided to call it a night and head back to my tent. Brad Burke, our outfitter, and a few of the fellow travelers went to check on the herd. They were rewarded. The still-drenched herd was standing across the spillway of what locals call Pine River but which modern maps refer to as Claire River. A brilliant, full moon hovered over a heavy mist-laden landscape. Even at that late hour, they saw calves romping and head butting, their brush with death not even a memory.

In the silence of that trip, with the suggestion that the predators were fewer than in years past, I felt I saw the natural rhythm of Wood Buffalo. Left alone to find its level, the system will change and adjust. Perhaps letting water back into the delta will help. I am confident that the air around Lousy Creek will echo once again with the music of the buffalo wolf. As long as we allow the system to find its own levels and adjustments, lows and highs will occur. Silent springs will be followed by the howling of wolf pups. The thunder of bison hooves and the grunting of cows calling for their calves will fill the air. Meadows will be trampled under bison hooves, and sharp-tailed grouse will dance anew. Soon enough the buffalo wolf will regain its numbers. And enough bison will stay just far enough out of reach to continue the dance of predator and prey through the decades and centuries. And we will all know that somewhere in a remote corner of Canada, without the further meddling of humans, an ancient rhythm continues much as it did when Columbus first walked upon the sands of Hispaniola. If other human priorities are set in place, then enlightenment, not agendas, should rule the day.

Selected References

Allison, L. "The Status of Bison on the Peace-Athabasca Delta."
   Canadian Wildlife Service Report, 1972.

Aniskowicz, B. J. "Life or Death? A Case for the Defense of Wood
   Buffalo National Park's Bison." *Nature Canada* (1990): 35–38.

Banfield, A. W. F., and N. S. Novakowski. "The Survival of the Wood
   Bison (*Bison bison athabascae* Rhoads) in the Northwest
   Territories." *National Museum of Canada Historical Papers* 8 (1960).

Bergman, C. M. "Behavioural Response to Resource Availability by
   Northern Ungulates." Ph.D. diss., University of Guelph, Guelph,
   Ont., 2000.

BERT (Bison Emergency Response Team). Parks Canada staff newslet-
   ter in response to FEARO recommendations, 1990.

Bradley, M. "Wood Buffalo National Park Bison Surveys, March 2002."
   Parks Canada Report, in preparation.

Broughton, E. "Diseases Affecting Bison." In *Bison Ecology in Relation to
   Agricultural Development in the Slave River Lowlands, N.W.T.,* ed. H.
   W. Reynolds and A. W. L. Hawley, 34–48. Canadian Wildlife
   Service, Occasional Paper 63, 1987.

Calef, G. W. "Population Growth in an Introduced Herd of Wood Bison." In *Northern Ecology and Resource Management,* ed. R. Olson, F. Geddes, and R. Hastings, 183–200. Edmonton: University of Alberta Press, 1984.

Carbyn, L. N. "Summary of Observations Obtained from Bison Surveys in the Mackenzie Bison Sanctuary near Fort Providence, N.W.T." Canadian Wildlife Service Report, 1968.

———. "Wolves and Bison in Wood Buffalo National Park, Past, Present, and Future." In *Buffalo,* ed. J. Foster, D. Harrison, and I. MacLaren, 167–78. Edmonton: University of Alberta Press, 1992.

Carbyn, L. N., N. Lunn, and K. Timoney. "Trends in the Distribution and Abundance of Bison in Wood Buffalo National Park." *Wildlife Society Bulletin* 26 (1998): 463–70.

Carbyn, L. N., S. M. Oosenbrug, and D. W. Anions. *Wolves, Bison, and the Dynamics Related to the Peace-Athabasca Delta in Canada's Wood Buffalo National Park.* Edmonton, Alberta: Canadian Circumpolar Institute, 1993.

Carbyn, L. N., and T. Trottier. "Descriptions of Wolf Attacks on Bison Calves in Wood Buffalo National Park." *Arctic* 41 (1988): 297–302.

———. "Responses of Bison on Their Calving Grounds to Predation by Wolves in Wood Buffalo National Park." *Canadian Journal of Zoology* 65 (1987): 2072–78.

Carbyn, L. N., and D. Watson. "Translocation of Plains Bison to Wood Buffalo National Park: Economic and Conservation Implications." In *Large Mammal Restoration,* ed. D. S. Maehr, R. F. Noss, and J. L. Larkin, 189–204. Washington, D.C.: Island Press, 2001.

Chalmers, J. W., et al., eds. *The Land of Peter Pond.* Edmonton, Alberta: Boreal Institute for Northern Studies, 1982.

Chisholm, J., L. Comin, and T. Unka. "Consensus-based Research to Assist with Bison Management in Wood Buffalo National Park." In *International Symposium on Bison Ecology and Herd Management in North America,* ed. L. Irby and J. Knight. Missoula: Montana State University, 1998.

Choquette, L. P. E. "Anthrax." In *Infectious Diseases of Wild Mammals,* ed. J. W. Davis, L. H. Karstad, and D. O. Trainer, 256–66. 1st ed. Ames: Iowa State University Press, 1970.

Choquette, L. P. E., E. Broughton, A. Currier, J. G. Cousineau, and N. S. Novakowski. "Parasites and Diseases of Bison in Canada." Part

3, "Anthrax Outbreaks in the Last Decade in Northern Canada and Control Measures." *Canadian Field-Naturalist* 86 (1972): 127–32.

Christopherson, R. G., R. G. Hudson, and M. K. Christopherson. "Seasonal Energy Expenditures and Thermoregulatory Responses of Bison and Cattle." *Canadian Journal of Animal Science* 59 (1979): 611–17.

Christopherson, R. G., R. G. Hudson, and R. G. Richmond. "Comparative Winter Bioenergetics of American Bison, Yak, Scottish Highland, and Hereford Calves." *Acta Theriologica* 23 (1978): 49–54.

Church, N. "Fur Harvest Survey, Wood Buffalo National Park." Canada Wildlife Service/Parks Canada Report, 1976.

Cooper, S. "Bison Range Situation and Flooding in the Peace-Athabasca Delta." Parks Canada Report, 1974.

Cortner, H. J., and M. Moote. *The Politics of Ecosystem Management.* Washington, D.C.: Island Press, 1999.

Crozier Information Resources Consulting and Synergy Canada. *Proceedings of the Workshop on the Bison Research Containment Program.* Parks Canada Workshop, Edmonton, Alberta, 1995.

Currier, A. A. "Report on the Buffalo Hunt, Wood Buffalo National Park, January 11–28, 1971." Canada Wildlife Service. Typescript, 1971.

Dekker, D. "Two Decades of Wildlife Investigations at Devona Jasper National Park, 1981–2001." Dick Dekker in collaboration with Wes Bradford and other park wardens. Parks Canada. Typescript, 2001.

Edmonton Journal. "Kill Park's Diseased Bison—Researcher," April 18, 2001.

Egerton, P. J. M. "The Cow-Calf Relationship and Rutting Behaviour in the American Bison." Master's thesis, University of Alberta, Edmonton, 1962.

FEARO. "Northern Diseased Bison Report of the Environmental Assessment Panel under the Federal Environmental Assessment and Review Process," Ottawa, Ont.: Government of Canada, 1990.

Ferguson, T. "Wood Bison and the Early Fur Trade." In *The Uncovered Past: Roots of Northern Alberta Societies,* ed. P. McCormack and R. Ironside, 63–79. Edmonton, Alberta: Circumpolar Institute, 1993.

Fuller, W. A. "Aerial Census of Northern Bison in Wood Buffalo National Park and Vicinity." *Journal of Wildlife Management* 14 (1950): 445–51.

————. "Behaviour and Social Organization of the Wild Bison of Wood Buffalo National Park, Canada." *Arctic* 13, no. 1 (1960): 3–19.

————. "The Biology and Management of Bison of Wood Buffalo National Park." *Wildlife Management Bulletin* ser. 1, no. 16 (1966).

————. "Canada and the Buffalo: A Tale of Two Herds." *Canadian Field-Naturalist* 114 (2002): 114–59.

————. "Disease Management in Wood Buffalo National Park Canada: Public Attitudes and Management Implications." In *Transactions of the Fifty-sixth North American Wildlife and Natural Resources Conference*, ed. R. E. McCabe, 50–55. Washington, D.C.: Wildlife Management Institute, 1991.

————. "The Ecology and Management of the American Bison." *Extrait de la Terre et la Vie* 2 (1961): 286–304.

————. "Report on the Buffalo Hunt, Wood Buffalo National Park." Parks Canada Report, 1952.

Fuller, W. A., and B. A. Hubert. "Fish, Fur, and Game in the Northwest Territories: Some Problems and Prospects for Increased Harvests." In *Proceedings of the First International Symposium on Renewable Resources and the Economy of the North*, 12–29. Ottawa: Association of Canadian Universities for Northern Studies, 1981.

Fuller, W. A., and G. H. LaRoi. "Historical Review of Biological Resources of the Peace-Athabasca Delta." In *Proceedings of the Peace-Athabasca Delta Symposium*, 153–73. Edmonton: Water Resources Center, University of Alberta, 1971.

Fuller, W. A., and N. Novakowski. "Wolf Control Operations, Wood Buffalo National Park, 1951–52." *Wildlife Management Bulletin* ser. 1, no. 11 (1955).

Gates, C., T. Chowns, and H. Reynolds. "Wood Buffalo at the Crossroads." In *Buffalo*, ed. J. Foster, D. Harrison, and I. MacLaren, 139–65. Edmonton: University of Alberta Press, 1992.

Gates, C., B. T. Elkin, and L. N. Carbyn. "The Diseased Bison Issue in Northern Canada." In *Brucellosis, Bison, Elk, and Cattle in the Greater Yellowstone Area: Defining the Problem, Exploring Solutions*, ed. E. T. Thorne, M. S. Boyce, P. Nicoletti, and T. Kreeger, 120–32. Cheyenne: Wyoming Game and Fish Department, 1997.

Gates, C., and N. C. Larter. "Growth and Dispersal of an Erupting Large Herbivore Population in Northern Canada: The Mackenzie Wood Bison *(Bison bison athabascae)*." *Arctic* 43 (1990): 231–38.

Gates, C., J. Mitchell, J. Wierzchowski, and L. Giles. "A Landscape
    Evaluation of Bison Movements and Distribution in Northern
    Canada." Typescript, 2001.

Geist, V. *Buffalo Nation: History and Legend of the North American Bison.*
    Stillwater, Minn.: Voyageur Press, 1996.

———. "Phantom Subspecies: The Wood Bison *Bison bison `athabascae'*
    Rhoads 1897 Is Not a Valid Taxon, but an Ecotype." *Arctic* 44
    (1991): 283–300.

Geist, V., and P. Karsten. "The Wood Bison (*Bison bison athabascae*
    Rhoads) in Relation to Hypotheses on the Origin of the American
    Bison (*Bison bison* Linnaeus)." *Zeitschrift fuer Saugetierkunde* 42
    (1977): 119–27.

Globe and Mail (Canada). "Action Imperative," letter to the editor,
    March 13, 1990.

Government of the Northwest Territories. "Mackenzie Wood Bison
    Management Plan." Yellowknife: Department of Renewable
    Resources, Government of the Northwest Territories, 1987.

Graham, M. "Finding Range for Canada's Buffalo." *Canadian Field-
    Naturalist* 38 (1924).

Gunn, L. *Thebacha Trails. A Guide to Special Areas around Fort Smith,
    N.W.T.* Winnipeg: Kromar Printing, 2000.

Gunson, J. "A Brief Wildlife Survey of the Athabasca-Peace Delta,
    Northern Alberta." Report for the International Biological
    Program. Typescript, 1969.

Harper, F. Letter to the Editor. *Canadian Field-Naturalist* 39 (1925): 45.

Hearne, S. *A Journey from Prince of Wales Fort in Hudson's Bay to the
    Northern Ocean.* London, Eng., 1795; Toronto, Champlain Society,
    1911.

Hediger, H. 1980. *Tiere verstehen, Erkenntnisse eines Tierpsychologen.*
    Munich: Kindler, 1980.

Hornaday, W. T. *The Extermination of the American Bison.* From *The Report
    of the National Museum, 1886–87,* 367–548. Washington, D.C.:
    Government Printing Office, 1889.

Hudson, R. J., T. Tennessen, and A. Sturko. "Behavioural and
    Physiological Reactions of Bison to Handling during an Anthrax
    Vaccination Program in Wood Buffalo National Park." In *Wood
    Buffalo National Park: Bison Research, 1972–76,* ed. G. Stelfox, G1–G21.
    Canadian Wildlife Service/Parks Canada Annual Report, 1976.

Hunt, B., ed. *Rebels, Rascals, and Royalty: The Colorful North of LACO Hunt.* Yellowknife, N.W.T.: Outcrop Publishing, 1983.

Joly, D. "Brucellosis and Tuberculosis as Factors Limiting Population Growth of Northern Bison." Ph.D. diss., University of Saskatchewan, Regina, 2001.

Komers, P. E., F. Messier, and C. Gates. "Group Structure in Wood Bison: Nutritional and Reproductive Determinants." *Canadian Journal of Zoology* 71 (1993): 1367–71.

———. "Search and Relax. The Case of Bachelor Wood Bison." *Behavioral Ecology and Sociobiology* 31, no. 3 (1992): 195–203.

Komers, P. E., F. Messier, P. F. Flood, and C. Gates. "Reproductive Behavior of Male Wood Bison in Relation to Progesterone Levels in Females." *Journal of Mammalogy* 75, no. 3 (1994): 757–65.

Kuyt, E. "Report on Bison Survey, Peace-Athabasca Delta." Canadian Wildlife Service. Typescript, 1971.

Larter, N. C., and C. Gates. "Diet and Habitat Selection of Wood Bison in Relation to Seasonal Changes in Forage Quantity and Quality." *Canadian Journal of Zoology* 69 (1991): 2677–85.

———. "Home Ranges of Wood Bison in an Expanding Population." *Journal of Mammalogy* 71 (1990): 604–7.

Mackenzie, A. *Voyages from Montreal on the River St. Lawrence through the Continent of North America, to the Frozen and Pacific Oceans, in the Years 1789 and 1793.* 1801; Toronto: Radisson Society of Canada, 1927.

McCormack, P. A. "The Political Economy of Bison Management in Wood Buffalo National Park." *Arctic* (1992): 367–80.

Meagher, M. M. "Range Extension by Bison of Yellowstone National Park." *Journal of Mammalogy* 70 (1989): 670–75.

Mech, L. D., R. E. McRobers, R. O. Peterson, and R. E. Page. "Relationship of Deer and Moose Populations to Previous Winter's Snow." *Journal of Animal Ecology* 56 (1987): 615–27.

Messier, F. "Effects of Bison Population Changes on Wolf-Prey Dynamics in and around Wood Buffalo National Park." In *Compendium of Government Submissions and Technical Specialists Reports*, 229–62. Vancouver, B.C.: Federal Environmental Review Office, 1989.

Morgan, R. G. "Bison Movement Patterns on the Canadian Plains, an Ecological Analysis." *Plains Anthropologist* 25 (1980): 143–60.

Nishi, J., T. Ellsworth, D. Balsillie, B. Elkin, G. Wilson, and J. van

Kessel. "An Overview of the Hook Lake Wood Bison Recovery
Project: Where Have We Come From, Where Are We Now, and
Where Would We Like to Go?" In *Second International Bison
Conference Proceedings,* 215–33. Edmonton, Alberta: Bison Center for
Excellence, 2001.

Novakowski, N. S. "Report on the Tagging, Testing, and Slaughtering
of Bison in the Lake Claire Area of Wood Buffalo National Park,
October–November 1957." Canadian Wildlife Service Report, 1958.

Novakowski, N. S., and L. P. E. Choquette. 1967. "Proposed Five-Year
Management Plan for Bison in Wood Buffalo National Park."
Canadian Wildlife Service. Typescript, 1967.

Nudds, T. D. "How Many Bison Should Be in Wood Buffalo National
Park?" *Canadian Field-Naturalist* 107 (1993): 117–19.

Olgilvie, S. C. "The Park Buffalo." National and Provincial Parks
Association of Canada, 1977.

Olson, B. E. "Wood Buffalo National Park Bison Round-up: Testing and
Slaughter Program, 1957–1958." Parks Canada Report. Typescript,
1958.

Peterson, M. J. "Wildlife Parasitism, Science, and Management Policy."
Journal of Wildlife Management 55 (1991): 782–89.

Popper, D. E., and F. J. Popper. "Great Plains: Checkered Past and
Hopeful Future." *Forum for Applied Research and Public Policy* (winter 1994): 89–100.

Preble, E. A. *A Biological Investigation of the Athabasca-Mackenzie Region.*
Washington, D.C.: Government Printing Office, 1908.

Raup, H. M. "Range Conditions in the Wood Buffalo Park of Western
Canada with Notes on the History of the Wood Bison." *Special
Publication of the American Commission on International Wildlife
Protection* 1, no. 2 (1933): 1–51.

Reynolds, H. W., R. M. Hansen, and D. G. Peden. "Diets of the Slave
River Lowlands Bison Herd, Northwest Territories, Canada."
Journal of Wildlife Management 42 (1978): 581–90.

Rhoads, S. M. "Notes on the Living and Extinct Species of North
American Bovidae." *Proceedings of the Academy of Natural Sciences
of Philadelphia* 49 (1897): 585–602.

Rich, E. E., ed. 1938. *Journal of Occurrences in the Athabasca Department
by George Simpson, 1820 and 1821, and Report.* Toronto: Champlain
Society, 1938. Reprint, Nendeln/Liechtenstein: Krause, 1968.

Salisbury, Michael. "Wolf." In *BBC Natural History Unit's Wildlife Specials*, ed. K. Scholey, 52–77. London: Trident Press, 1999.

Schneider, Richard. "Bison-Wolf Dynamics in Northern Canada: A Simulation Study." Typescript, 1997.

Sinclair, A. R. E. *The African Buffalo: A Study of Resource Limitation of Populations.* Chicago: University of Chicago Press, 1977.

Soper, D. "History, Range, and Home of the Northern Bison." *Ecological Monographs* 2 (1941): 347–412.

———. "Mammals of Wood Buffalo National Park, Northern Alberta, and District of Mackenzie." *Journal of Mammalogy* 23, no. 3 (1942): 119–45.

———. "Report on Wildlife Investigations in Wood Buffalo National Park and Vicinity, Alberta and Northwest Territories, Canada." Canadian Wildlife Service, Report 252, 1945.

Stelfox, J. G., ed. *Wood Buffalo National Park: Bison Research, 1977.* Canadian Wildlife Service/Parks Canada Annual Report, 1977.

Stephenson, R. O., S. Gerlach, R. D. Guthrie, C. R. Harrington, R. O. Mills, and G. Hare. "Wood Bison in Late Holocene Alaska and Adjacent Canada: Paleontological, Archeological, and Historical Records." In *People and Wildlife in Northern North America: Essays in Honor of R. Dale Guthrie*, 124–58. Oxford: Archaeopress, 2001.

Struzik, E. "The Last Buffalo Slaughter." *Canadian Forum* no. 794 (1990): 6–11.

Telfer, E., and J. Kelsall. "Studies of Morphological Parameters Affecting Ungulate Locomotion in Snow." *Canadian Journal of Zoology* 57 (1979): 2153–59.

Tessaro, S. V. "A Descriptive and Epizootiological Study of Brucellosis and Tuberculosis in Bison in Northern Canada." Ph.D. diss., University of Saskatchewan, Regina, 1987.

Truett, J. C., M. Phillips, K. Kunkle, and R. Miller. "Managing Bison to Restore Biodiversity." *Great Plains Research* 11 (2001): 123–44.

Van Camp, J. "Snow Conditions and the Winter Feeding Behavior of *Bison bison* in Elk Island National Park." Canadian Wildlife Service Report. Typescript, 1975.

———. "A Surviving Herd of Endangered Wood Bison at Hook Lake, N.W.T." *Arctic* 42 (1989): 314–22.

Van Camp, J., and R. Gluckie. "A Record Long-Distance Move by a Wolf *(Canis lupus).*" *Journal of Mammalogy* 60 (1979): 236.

Van Kessel, J. "Taking Care of Bison: Community Perception of the Hook Lake Wood Bison Recovery Project in Fort Resolution, N.T., Canada." Master's thesis, University of Alberta, Edmonton, 2002.

Van Zyll de Jong, C. G. "A Systematic Study of Recent Bison with Particular Consideration of the Wood Bison *(Bison bison athabascae)* Rhoads 1897." National Museum of Canada, Report, Ser. 6, 1986.

Westworth Associates Environmental Consultants. *An Environmental Assessment of a Proposed Winter Road in Wood Buffalo National Park.* Westworth Associates Report, 2000.

Wobeser, G. "Disease in Northern Bison: What to Do? A Personal Perspective." In *Buffalo,* ed. J. Foster, D. Harrison, and I. MacLaren, 179–88. Edmonton: University of Alberta Press, 1992.

Wood Bison Recovery Team. *Status Report on Endangered Wildlife in Canada, 1987: Wood Bison.* Ottawa, Ont.: Canadian Wildlife Service, 1987.

Wood Buffalo National Park. "Bison Movement and Distribution Study: Final Report." *Technical Report 94-08WB.* Fort Smith, N.W.T.: Wood Buffalo National Park, 1995.

Young, S. P., and E. A. Goldman. *The Wolves of North America.* Washington, D.C.: American Wildlife Institute, 1944.

Index

The text is set in 11.25/15 Monotype Dante, a font originally designed as a hot-metal typeface. Giovani Mardersteig's intent was to create a roman and italic that would work together harmoniously—not unlike the interrelationship of the buffalo wolf and bison. The display font is Gargoyle Medium.

The text was typeset in-house by the designer. The book was printed on 50# Maple Eggshell Shade 86 at the Maple-Vail Book Manufacturing Group in York, Pa. The cover was printed at Lehigh Press, Inc., in Pennsauken, N.J.